Global Stage

Language Book 6

Elaine Boyd and Araminta Crace

macmillan education

Scope and Sequence

Unit	Vocabulary	Explore Language	Global Citizenship
Language Review	**Vocabulary** *Emotions; Crime; Nature; Being Eco-Friendly; Storytelling; Work and Skills* **Grammar** *Present Perfect; Tag Questions; Present and Past Passive; Too and Enough; Agreeing with Too, So, Either, and Neither; Reported Speech; First and Second Conditional*		
1 Keep in Touch page 10	**Technology** *blog, blog post, comment, crash, download, email, message, save to favorites, search history, upload* **Online Safety** *create a profile, devices, lowercase letters, online privacy, online safety, password, personal information, register, secure, special characters, uppercase letters, username* **Chant** *Search the Net*	Verbs of Thinking Simple and Progressive Forms	How does technology help us learn? **Listening Skills** Listening for gist and details
2 Time for a Change page 22	**Lifestyle and Habits** *argue, be late, healthy diet, junk food, messy, polite, punctual, workout, rude, sleep late* **Healthy Food** *convenience food, high in fiber, high in salt and sugar, in season, local produce, packaging, processed food, red meat, saturated fat, white meat, whole grains* **Poem** *You Can Do Better*	Present Perfect Present Perfect Progressive	How do eating habits affect our lives? **Listening Skills** Listening for gist and details
Put It Together	**Review Units 1 and 2** ***Know It, Win It***		
3 Dream Big page 36	**Dreams and Ambitions** *ambition, confidence, determination, happiness, health, pride, success, wealth* **Persevering to Succeed** *be the hero, do things for fun, experience failure, fear of the unknown, find joy in, fresh start, notice the small things, nurture friendship* **Poem** *My Dreams*	Second Conditional *Wish* + Past Forms	How can children help solve the world's problems? **Listening Skills** Listening for gist and details
4 How's That Possible? page 48	**Facts, Mysteries, and Illusions** *evidence, fact, have a feeling, make up, optical illusion, play a trick, puzzle, see things* **Historical Discoveries** *ancient monument, archaeologist, clue, expert, legend, prehistoric times, solve, theory* **Poem** *My Friend Oscar*	Modals of Deduction: Past Forms Modals of Obligation: Past Forms	Why is it important to explore things we don't understand? **Listening Skills** Listening for gist and details
Put It Together	**Review Units 3 and 4** ***Chatter Boxes***		
5 What Is Art? page 62	**Describing Paintings** *abstract shapes, complex, doodles, dots, lines, playful, powerful, serious, simple, squiggles* **Artistic Elements and Features** *contrast, creativity, depict, iconic, large-scale, masterpiece, style, symbolize* **Poem** *The More I Look—A Poem Inspired by Kandinsky*	Past Perfect and Past Perfect Progressive Narrative Tenses	What can art tell us about different countries and periods of time? **Listening Skills** Listening for gist and details

Writing	Speaking	International English	Literacy Book
			Literacy: *Making Predictions; Sequence of Events; Sensory Details; Synonyms; Making Inferences; Understanding the Main Idea and Details; Transition Words*
Paragraph and Sentence Building Presenting Facts and Giving Details, Examples, and Opinions **Product** A Fact-Based Article	**Conversation** Asking for Clarification and Confirming Understanding **Pronunciation** Sentence Stress: Content Words	**US** *I forgot; take a look* **UK** *I've forgotten; have a look*	**Story** *Urgent Message* **Informational Text** *Communication Time* **Reading Skill** Understanding Chronology
Function Making Connections Between Entries **Word Study** Using Informal and Emotive Language **Product** A Diary Entry	**Presentation** Supporting an Argument and Being Persuasive **Pronunciation** Sentence Stress: Weak Forms	**US** *messy; we've gotten better* **UK** *untidy; we've got better*	**Diary** *My Stay at Camp Karma* **Informational Text** *Why Do We Sleep?* **Reading Skill** Analyzing and Evaluating
Paragraph Building Describing Causes and Effects, and Suggesting Solutions **Word Study** Positive and Negative Adjectives **Product** A Cause and Effect Article	**Conversation** Asking for Ideas and Summarizing Points **Pronunciation** Connected Speech: Consonant-Vowel Linking	**US** *soccer uniform* **UK** *football kit*	**Creative Nonfiction** *Communities Making Dreams Come True* **Poem** *Dreams* **Reading Skill** Understanding Author's Word Choice
Paragraph Building Including and Omitting Information **Word Study** Review: Time Phrases and Adjectives about Feelings and Reactions **Product** A Story Beginning	**Presentation** Asking Questions and Pausing for Effect **Pronunciation** Connected Speech: Elision, Dropping the *t*		**Informational Text** *The Sci-Files* **Fantasy** *An Enlightening Journey* **Reading Skill** Making Inferences
Paragraph Building Linking the Beginning, Middle, and End of a Story **Word Study** Using Descriptive Language **Product** A Mini Saga	**Presentation** Organizing and Summarizing Points **Pronunciation** Sentence Stress: Content Words	**US** *leaned* **UK** *leant*	**Creative Nonfiction** *Cave Painting* **Folk Tale** *The Boy Who Drew Cats* **Reading Skill** Recognizing Genres

Unit	Vocabulary	Explore Language	Global Citizenship
6 It's Your Turn page 74	**Playing Traditional Board Games** *board game, chance, land on, lose, miss a turn, pieces, players, strategy, throw the dice, win* **Playing Video Games** *avatar, collaborate, collect points, gaming, graphics, instructions, level up, multiplayer, role-playing game, virtual* **Poem** *Fun and Games*	Indirect Questions Defining and Non-defining Relative Clauses	How can games help you learn about other ways of life? **Listening Skills** Listening for gist and details
Put It Together	**Review Units 5 and 6** *Yesterday's Vacation Fun*		
7 All About Ads page 88	**Advertising** *advertisement, bargain, billboard, customer, discount, persuade, products, profit, quality, value* **Branding in Advertising** *brand, claims, false impression, image, promote, slogan, small print, target market* **Chant** *Why Buy?*	Reported Speech: Statements and Commands Reported Speech: Questions	What do advertisements sell, other than products? **Listening Skills** Listening for gist and details
8 What Are the Odds? page 100	**Numbers, Shapes, and Symmetry** *angle, divide, even number, hexagon, multiply, odd number, prime number, sequence, spirals, symmetry* **Statistics Descriptors** *average, chart, data, fall, percentage, reach a peak, rise, statistics, stay stable, trend* **Poem** *I Love Numbers*	Passives: Present and Past Passives: Future Forms *Will, Going to*	How does math link to different aspects of our lives? **Listening Skills** Listening for gist and details
Put It Together	**Review Units 7 and 8** *Word Scramble Race*		
9 Make Up Your Mind page 114	**Decision-making** *brainstorm the options, consider the consequences, decide on a solution, define the problem, evaluate your ideas, learn from your mistakes, make a decision, regret* **Collaborative Decision-making** *be fair, control your emotions, fit in with, get your own way, have your say, independence, individual identity, peer pressure, pros and cons* **Poem** *Make Up My Mind*	Third Conditional: Statements Third Conditional: Questions	How do the decisions we make affect other people? **Listening Skills** Listening for gist and details
10 Take the Lead page 126	**Positive Values** *can-do attitude, encourage, gut feeling, inspire, mentor, positive influence, respect, role model* **Influencing and Leading** *commitment, focus, honest, motivate, organizational skills, passionate, set a good example, support* **Poem** *Let's Look to the Future*	Future Progressive Review: Future Forms	Can anyone be a leader? **Listening Skills** Listening for gist and details
Put It Together	**Review Units 9 and 10** *Solve a Problem!*		
Process Writing page 140	**Generating Ideas** Step 1 **Planning** Step 2	**Drafting** Step 3 **Editing and Publishing** Step 4	

Writing	Speaking	International English	Literacy Book
Function Introducing Ideas and Making Comparisons **Word Study** Using Adverb and Adjective Collocations **Product** A For and Against Article	**Conversation** Giving Opinions and Disagreeing **Pronunciation** Intonation in Exclamations		**Informational Text** *The History of Board Games* **Story** *The Game of Life* **Reading Skill** Understanding Denotation and Connotation
Paragraph Building Giving Reasons and Summarizing Ideas **Word Study** Using Adjectives to Reinforce Opinion **Product** An Opinion Essay	**Conversation** Preparing for an Interview; Describing Qualities, Skills, and Experience **Pronunciation** Intonation	**US** *donut, advertisement* **UK** *doughnut, advert*	**Science Fiction** *Commercial Break* **Persuasive Text** *Ad Smart* **Reading Skill** Identifying Text and Graphic Features
Paragraph Building Writing Chronologically and Supporting a Point with Examples **Product** A Biography	**Presentation** Engaging and Motivating Your Audience; Using Visuals **Pronunciation** Consonant clusters	**US** *analyzed* **UK** *analysed*	**Biography** *Ada Lovelace* **Story** *The Binary Life* **Reading Skill** Recognizing Story Structure
Function Organizing Information and Engaging the Reader **Product** An Instructional Article	**Conversation** Inviting Contributions to a Conversation **Pronunciation** Connected Speech: Linking	**US** *middle school/high school; schedule* **UK** *secondary school; timetable*	**Instructional Text** *Making Decisions* **Story** *It's Not OK* **Reading Skill** Identifying Internal and External Conflict
Function Features of a Blog **Word Study** Informal Language and Ellipsis **Product** A Blog Post	**Presentation** Using Cause-and-effect Reasoning; Sounding Positive **Pronunciation** Sentence Stress: Influencing Meaning	**US** *regular people; buddy* **UK** *ordinary people; mate*	**Play** *Click to Follow* **Informational Text** *Recycle Runway* **Reading Skill** Summarizing Readings

A Listen and write. How did all the children feel?

1 confused
2 ______
3 ______
4 ______
5 ______
6 ______

B Unscramble and write the crime words.

1 fehit t hief
2 vticeedte d______
3 rineginrfpt f______
4 ciusiusspo s______
5 ulec c______
6 nstwsie w______

C Find and write five positive words and five negative words about nature and the environment.

Positive	Negative
1 e co-friendly	6 p ______
2 c ______	7 p ______
3 o ______	8 d ______
4 s ______	9 h ______
5 r ______	10 e ______

M R A H A Q D D G O P Y
S U S T A I N A B L E F
C O N S E R V A T I O N
E C O F R I E N D L Y R
C I N A G R O O K P P E
E N D A N G E R E D O C
N O I T U L L O P P I Y
E G A M A D R H M S S C
O M R R X U W I Q S O L
A D S J X I S X P J N E

D Read and complete.

fascinating **moral** **empathize** **suspense** **enemy** **imagination** **villain** ~~**character**~~ **hero**

I saw a great movie yesterday. The main 1 character was a man called Kasper, a brave 2 ______ trying to stop his worst 3 ______ ; a cruel 4 ______ who was controlling people's minds and taking away their 5 ______ and their ability to 6 ______ with other people who needed help. This 7 ______ movie, was full of 8 ______ but the 9 ______ of the story was that good always wins in the end!

E Look, read, and choose.

1 I'd really like to keep in touch with the stressful / (talented) friends I made at summer camp this year.

2 Doing our community project was a really rewarding / reliable experience—I felt really proud.

3 Pet psychologists have to be very independent / observant.

4 Snowboarding was very resourceful / challenging at first, but I worked hard and really improved.

5 I haven't worked as a party planner before, but I know I have the skills / experience for the job.

6 You need a degree / business to become an architect.

Language Review

A Listen and complete.

B Read and complete.

1 These drums were made (make) in Ghana.

2 I ____________ (teach) how to make sushi at the Japanese stall.

3 The Pyramids of the Sun and the Moon ____________ (build) about 2,000 years ago.

4 Indian food ____________ (eat) by millions of people every day.

5 This photo ____________ (take) on my new phone.

6 Chess ____________ (play) in many after-school clubs in Russia.

7 These poems ____________ (write) by children in Egypt.

8 All this food ____________ (prepare) by my family.

C Match the sentences to the responses.

1 I love chess! — b
2 I'm not hungry.
3 I didn't play the flute.
4 I'm too small to reach the top shelf.
5 I don't have enough money to buy it.
6 I wasn't good enough to win.

a. I don't either.
b. Me, too.
c. Neither was I.
d. Neither am I.
e. So am I.
f. I didn't either.

Grammar Present Perfect; Tag Questions; Present and Past Passive; *Too* and *Enough*; Agreeing with *Too*, *So*, *Either*, and *Neither*; Reported Speech; First and Second Conditional

D **Read and choose.**

1 a. Look at the girl (who) / what's wearing a soccer shirt.

   b. What did she say? She said that she loves / loved chess.

2 a. Look at the boys who / where are near the sushi stall.

   b. What did the boys say? They said they aren't / weren't hungry.

3 a. Look at the shelf who / where the dolls are.

   b. What did the girl say? She told the boy she was too small / small enough to reach the doll.

4 a. Look at the stall who / that's selling camels.

   b. What did the man say? He said he didn't have too / enough money.

E **Complete with the correct form of the verbs.**

Caleb: I 1 was thinking (think) about joining a new club when I saw the notice about the Guitar Club. You're a member, aren't you?

Ethan: Yes, and if you 2 ________ (join) the club, you'll make lots of new friends.

Caleb: I was walking to school this morning when I 3 ________ (see) my cousin Alex. She said she 4 ________ (want) to join, too.

Ethan: That's great. If I 5 ________ (be) you, I'd bring her to the meeting tonight. If she came with you, it 6 ________ (be) a great help as you could practice together. But even if you came alone, you 7 ________ (not be) on your own for long. If you 8 ________ (arrive) early you might hear Jessica playing at the end of her individual lesson. She's amazing!

Caleb: How much does it cost?

Ethan: You 9 ________ (not have to) pay to join the club—it's free.

UNIT 1

Keep in Touch

A Listen. What information does Daniel want? How does he find it?

- ☐ blog
- ☐ blog post
- ☐ comment
- 1 crash
- ☐ download
- ☐ email
- ☐ message
- ☐ save to favorites
- ☐ search history
- ☐ upload

B Find and number the words in **A**. Then listen and check.

C Close your eyes. Listen, visualize, and say.

D Look and write. There is more than one possible answer.

Getting information, photos, and videos	Writing information and showing photos and videos	Having a problem
	blog, blog post	

E Listen and write. Then watch and say.

Search the Net

Search the net, search the net.
My turn to search and write the
1 b<u>log</u> p<u>ost</u> !

Search the net, search the net.
Facts—who can find the most?

Search the net, search the net.
2 S__________ to favorites now!

Search the net, search the net.
3 U__________ your photos—wow!

Search the net, search the net.
Don't 4 d__________ that—it's trash!

Search the net, search the net.
My computer's going to 5 c__________ !

F Pronunciation. Listen and say. Copy the sentence stress. Find other sentences in the poem and notice the stress patterns.

My turn to search and write the blog post!

Save to favorites now!

My computer's going to crash!

Explore Language

A Listen and read. What's different about a school day in Ghana?

Daniel: Hey Deepak—I have a lot of facts about Ghana for our blog. Did you know that the official language is English?

Deepak: Interesting. What else did you find out?

Daniel: Well, I read on one boy's blog that schoolchildren can get up between 5:30 and 6 o'clock—before it's too hot. This boy I read about gets up at 4:30.

Deepak: 4:30! I wonder if he always wakes up on time—I don't know if I could do that.

Daniel: Before school, children usually clean the house, fetch water, or help prepare the evening meal. They make their own breakfast, too.

Deepak: Wow! Do you know how they get to school?

Daniel: Most children walk—sometimes for an hour. When it's time for class, drums start playing.

Deepak: Drums? I don't understand why they have drums.

Daniel: To get everyone excited about the school day, I guess! But I don't remember if the children play them. Let's look ... Oh, I forgot which website it was.

Deepak: Did you save it to favorites?

Daniel: Yes ... here it is! I wonder whether we'll go into class playing music some day.

🇺🇸	🇬🇧
I forgot	I've forgotten

B Look at **A**. Complete the table. What verb forms can follow *if* or *wh–* words?

Verbs of Thinking

	______			he always wakes up on time.
I	______	remember	if/whether	the children play them.
	______			we'll go into class playing music some day.
I	______		which	website it was.
	don't	______	______	they have drums.

✔ *I don't remember.*
✘ ~~*I'm not remembering.*~~
Remember

C Think and discuss. Then choose.

1 We can use *if* and *whether* after a verb of thinking when the answer to the question is *yes or no* / *a specific detail*.

2 We use a *wh– word* / *if or whether* after a verb of thinking when we're considering *who*, *where*, *what*, *why*, or *how*.

D Listen and say.

E Read and complete the sentences with the correct word.

1 I forgot __what__ the homework is.

2 I can remember ______ all my friends' birthdays are.

3 I wonder ______ I'll get many comments on my blog.

4 I don't understand ______ the internet works.

5 I don't know ______ I'll go to college in the future.

6 I wonder ______ I'll be able to finish my homework on time.

7 I'm not sure ______ time the school play starts.

8 I wonder ______ I have so many emails.

F Think and discuss. Are the sentences in **E** true for you?

I didn't forget what the homework is. I already finished it.

I didn't forget either. I'm going to do it after school.

How does technology help us learn?

A Listen to an online video tutorial. What information does the tutorial give?

put your name and other information on an official list	control over what information you give about yourself over the internet	being or staying safe when connected to the internet	post personal details and other information on on a website or app
1 register	2 ______	3 ______	4 ______

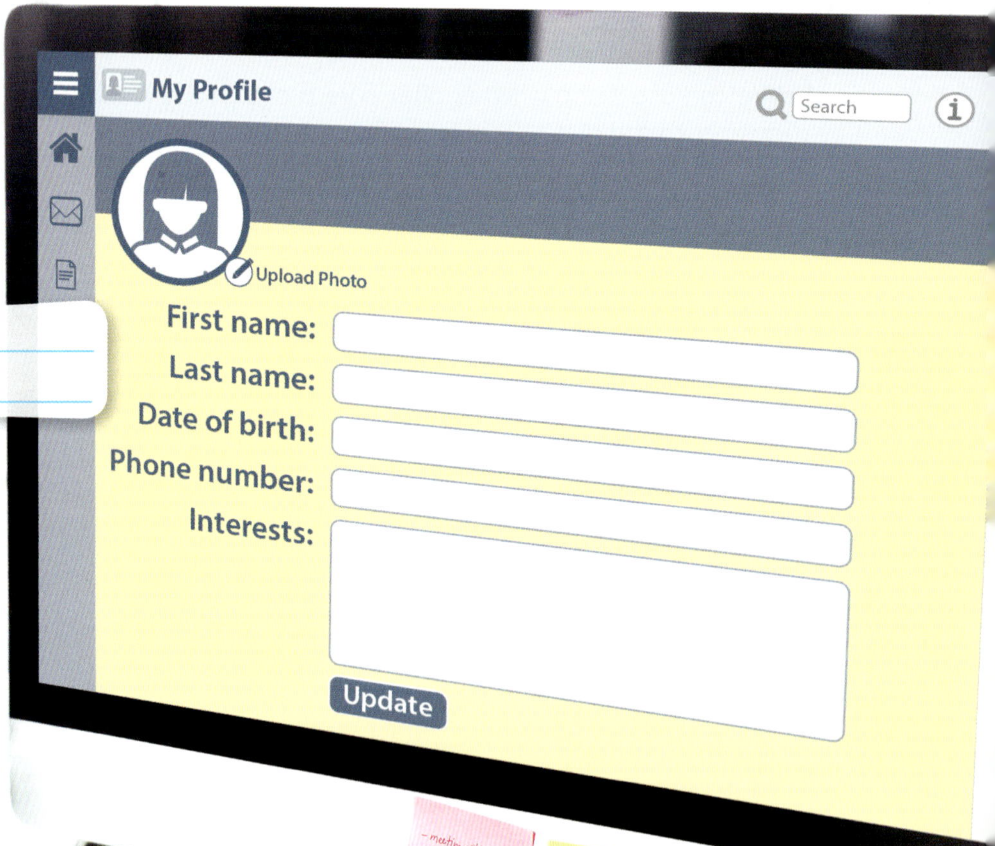

5 ______

6 ______

7 ______

Lisa_Lemon28	p•••••••7	ARQTSE
8 ______	9 ______	10 ______

arqtse	*£$%&
11 ______	12 ______

B Look at the pictures and definitions in **A** and write. Then listen and check.

create a profile	devices	lowercase letters	online privacy
online safety	password	personal information	~~register~~
secure	special characters	uppercase letters	username

C Read and complete the online safety rules.

Rules For Online Safety

- Always check for signs that the website is 1 __secure__ . Does the address start with "https"? Is there a padlock symbol? Check quality: are there spelling mistakes on the site?
- Many websites, such as video-sharing websites, ask you to 2 ________ . Remember to ask your teacher, parent, or guardian first. It's important to protect your online 3 ________ .
- If you want to join one of these websites, you need to 4 ________ for yourself. Make your 5 ________ different from your real name. Maybe invent something funny!
- Choose a 6 ________ that no one else can guess. Use a special combination of uppercase and 7 ________ letters and numbers. It's a good idea to use some 8 ________ too, like *, $, and %.
- Always log out of a website when you've finished, especially if you are on a shared 9 ________ that other people use.
- Never give your 10 ________ without checking that it's safe to do so.

D Now listen to Pablo and Mari presenting a podcast. What's the podcast about?

E Listen again. Write *True*, *False*, or *Doesn't Say*.

1. Pablo is presenting the second part of a podcast. __True__
2. Mari thinks that all websites are worth reading. ________
3. Children in different countries think differently about some things. ________
4. Online study groups are only for studying school subjects. ________
5. There is information about the blog for parents. ________

How is technology a part of your everyday life?
What are the benefits and dangers of posting online?

Explore Language

A Listen and read. What does Sofia want? Can she have them?

Sofia: Deepak, did you know you can get selfie shoes? You put your phone in a special shoe and use your foot to take a selfie!

Deepak: Really, Sofia? Are you sure that's true?

Sofia: Yes! Daniel told me about it. When he was looking for information yesterday on how to take the best selfie, he found an article about it. He wasn't joking!

Deepak: Do you remember what Miss Goran said about checking for fake news?

Sofia: Oh, yeah—I forgot.

Deepak: Do you have the website there?

Sofia: Yes, I'm taking a look right now. What did Miss Goran tell us to check? Oh, yeah! Is anyone else reporting it?

Deepak: Yes. And also to check for things like bad spelling or grammar—is it bad quality?

Sofia: Well, yes, it is. While I was reading it, I found a lot of mistakes.

Deepak: Wait a minute. Look, it says here that the reports are fake!

Sofia: Well, I still want some. They'd be a great invention!

🇺🇸	🇬🇧
take a look	have a look

B Look at **A**. Complete the table. Which verbs are used to form questions?

Simple and Progressive Forms

It	______	here that the reports are fake!	
Daniel	______	me about it.	
Do	you	remember	what Miss Goran said?
I	______	taking	a look right now.
He	was	______	for information yesterday.
______	anyone else	reporting	it?

Remember

Use contractions
He's joking. / He isn't joking. / He wasn't joking.

C Think and discuss. Then match.

1 Simple present
2 Simple past
3 Present progressive
4 Past progressive

a. describes an action that is happening now or around now.
b. describes a long action in the past.
c. describes a present state or a habit.
d. describes a finished action in the past.

D Listen and say.

E Complete the sentences with the correct form of the verbs.

1 I was checking (check) my emails when Harper called. She
2 ______ (not remember) the website address we found yesterday. Do you have it?

3 ______ (you watch) TV right now? There's a great program about fake news on Channel 6.

4 ______ (you go) to the photography club on Saturday mornings?

5 My mom ______ (drive) me home from the mall when I dropped my phone out of the car window.

6 I ______ (take) a great photo but the screen cracked!

F Show a photo. Say when you took it, what you were doing, and how you feel when you look at it.

I took this photo when I was traveling in Norway last year ...

Write About It

A Read the article. Check (✓) the topics and opinions about using the internet that the writer discusses.

1 ◯ How many young people use it
2 ◯ How many old people use it
3 ◯ The good things
4 ◯ The dangers

Wow, The Internet Appeared!

About one in three children worldwide use the internet. A survey by *Global Kids Online* shows that many children think the internet is a necessity. Most children say the two best things about the internet are first, learning and second, being in touch with people.

The main things children like about learning online are: doing research for school and sharing their learning, having the freedom to learn new things, for example, the guitar, and listening to music online (using music websites, like Spotify).

Children like being in touch online firstly because they can contact friends or family who live far away, by email or video call. Secondly, they like sharing things, such as photos and videos they've made, and lastly, they like playing online games with friends.

There are some risks with using the internet. We must check for fake news and be careful about giving personal information. But I think this 15-year-old boy from the survey is right when he says, "We grew up with the internet … The grown-ups are like 'Wow, the internet appeared,' while it is perfectly normal for us." In my view, the internet is an essential part of our lives—after all, we don't know what life is like without it!

Talking to Mom

B Look at the structure of the article. Read and answer the questions.

1 How many paragraphs are there and what does each paragraph do? Four

2 Which come first: facts or opinions? ______

3 How does the writer give details? ______

4 How does the writer add interest? ______

C Look at the language in the article. Read and complete the table.

Giving opinions ~~Presenting facts~~ Giving examples Giving details

Presenting facts			
A survey shows … Most children say …	First, … second, … third, … Firstly, … secondly, … lastly, …	for example, like, such as,	In my view, I think

Process Writing
Generating Ideas, p140

D Think and discuss. How do you and your friends use the internet? Complete the mind map with your ideas and research.

Internet Activity	Reason or Example	Facts or Statistics
to look for new games	more games available online than in stores	91% of children in USA play video games

E Plan your article. Look at your ideas in **D**. Think of a title and make notes for each paragraph.

Title:
Introduction:
First main point (including facts):
Second main point (including facts):
Conclusion (including opinion):

F Now write your article. Include a photo.

Read and Respond
Ask your friend to read your article. Can he/she think of a fact or opinion to add?

Talk About It

A Watch and listen. What tasks do Gene and Lloyd each agree to do?

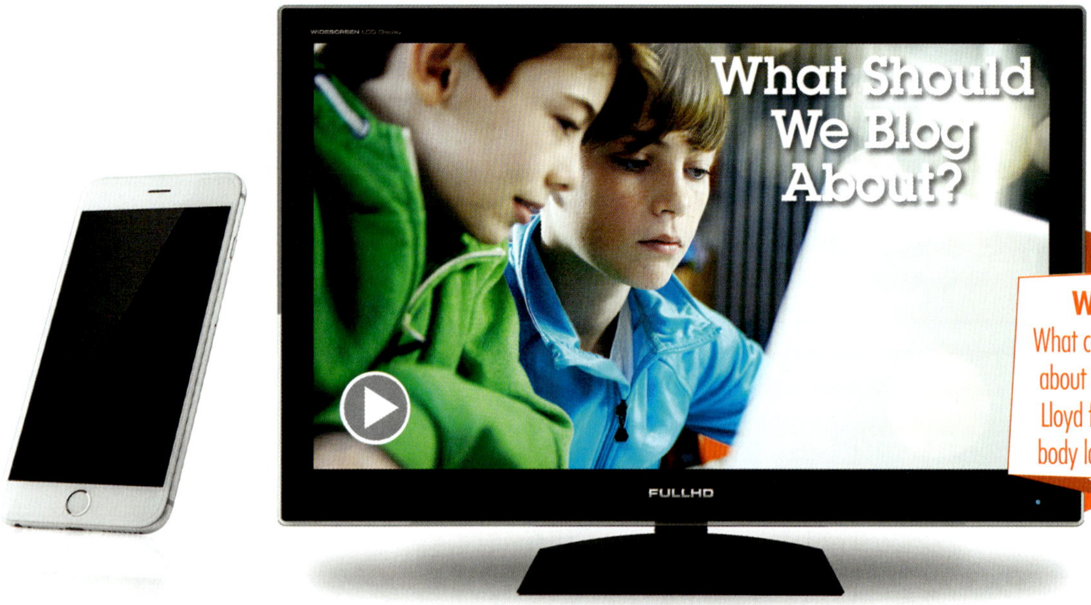

Watch
What can you tell about Gene and Lloyd from their body language?

B Watch again. Put the phrases in order. Write ***AC*** (asking for clarification) or ***CU*** (confirming understanding).

a. ☐ Yes, exactly! ________

b. ☐ Do you mean …? ________

c. ☐ That's right. ________

d. 1 What do you mean? AC

e. ☐ That's true. ________

f. ☐ So, you're saying …? ________

C Imagine you're going to create a blog post in groups. Think about these questions.

- What would you like to create a blog post about?
- What different tasks do you need to do?
- How will you decide who does each task and why?

D Talk with your friend, using phrases from **B**. Discuss your ideas for the blog post.

We could do something about cooking and food.

We need someone to upload some photos.

How about you do the writing?

Reflect
Did I ask for clarification?
Did I confirm understanding?

How well did you meet the challenge of Unit 1? Read and respond.

My Planning Sheet

We're all good at some things.
I'm good at …

And we all need to improve some things.
I need to work on …

We can always work to improve. Even when we are good at something, we can get better!
My plan to improve my English is …

If my plan works, then I'll …

I'll know my plan is working when …

UNIT 2 Time for a Change

A Listen. What are the rules for the sports club?

- [ ] argue
- [1] be late
- [ ] healthy diet
- [ ] junk food
- [ ] messy
- [ ] polite
- [ ] punctual
- [ ] work out
- [ ] rude
- [ ] sleep late

B Find and number the words in A. Then listen and check.

C Close your eyes. Listen, visualize, and say.

D Look and write. Then put the good habits in order of importance for you (1 = most important).

Be the Best! My Action Plan		
My bad habits	New good habits	
a. junk food	Eat more vegetables and fruit to have a ______.	☐
b. ______	Think about other people's feelings and be ______.	☐
c. ______	Go to bed and get up earlier so I can ______ before school.	☐
d. ______	Listen and respect others, and try to reach agreement.	☐
e. ______	Allow enough time to prepare things so I can be ______.	☐
f. ______	Put clothes away every day.	☐

E Listen and write. Then watch and say.

You Can Do Better

My brother said it wasn't great
That my room's a mess and I'm
1 sleeping late.
He tells me that I'm always 2 ______
And I'll get sick from all that
3 ______.

My brother says, "Don't 4 ______, keep
it cool,
You can do better, don't be a fool."

So I guess I have to try
To wave my bad habits all goodbye.

So I have a plan—but keep it quiet
5 ______ often, have a
6 ______,
Be 7 ______, 8 ______—I agree
To be the best that I can be.

messy (US) | untidy (UK)

F Pronunciation. Listen and say. Copy the weak forms. Find other examples in the poem.

You can /kən/ do better | I have to /tə/ try | To be the /ðə/ best

Explore Language

A Listen and read. Do Ziad and Isabella agree?

1

Ziad: Look at this debate, Diego. Have you ever been in one? I'm going to take part because I think the way we use technology has made us rude.

Diego: Do you think so? Has technology really changed the way we communicate?

Ziad: Yes, it has! People argue more now because they just say what they want online. Because they don't say it face-to-face, they don't think about the effect their words have on people.

Isabella: Well, I haven't become ruder. I think we've gotten better at communicating because technology lets us stay in touch. Like messaging someone to say happy birthday.

2

3

🇺🇸	🇬🇧
we've gotten better	we've got better

Ziad: OK, Isabella, but we've just seen someone being pretty rude, haven't we?

Isabella: What do you mean?

Diego: Well, when Coach García posted a notice about practice a few minutes ago, someone wrote "That's crazy! Do we have to start SO early?"

Isabella: OK. That doesn't sound very polite ... Is Coach García angry?

Ziad: I don't think so. He's already responded with "You snooze, you lose!"

B Look at **A**. Complete the table. What kinds of words come before the past participle?

Present Perfect

Have	you	______	been	in one?		
______	technology	really	______	the way we communicate?		
We	've	______	______	someone being pretty rude,	______	we?
He	______	______	responded.			

Remember

She's been = she went and came back.
She's gone = she hasn't come back.

C Think and discuss. Then choose.

1 We use the present perfect / simple past to talk about life experiences and things that happened before now.

2 We use the present perfect to talk about activities that started in the past and are finished / unfinished.

3 We can use *just*, *yet*, and *already* to give more information about when / why these activities happened.

D Listen and say.

E Complete with the present perfect.

1 What's the furthest you've ever run (ever run)?

2 ______ anyone ______ (ever be) rude to you?

3 ______ you ______ (change) your diet recently?

4 ______ any of your friends ______ (ever go) abroad?

5 Naomi ______ (already finish) the activity!

6 Miss Lucy ______ (just ask) me to encourage the other students to be punctual.

7 ______ your brother ______ (stop) eating junk food yet?

8 They ______ (not tell) the coach they can't come to practice yet. That's so rude!

F Ask and answer questions 1–4 in **E**. Then ask three new questions. Use time expressions in your answers.

What's the furthest you've ever run?

I've run ten kilometers. I took part in a fun run last month.

How do eating habits affect our lives?

A Listen to Victor talk to his dad. What changes is Victor's dad making to their meals?

1 in season

2 ______________

3 ______________

4 ______________

5 ______________

6 ______________

7 ______________

8 ______________

9 ______________

large amounts of the parts of fruit, vegetables, and grains that you cannot digest

10 ______________

foods that have chemicals or other substances added to keep them fresh for a long time

11 ______________

B Look at the pictures and definitions in **A** and write. Then listen and check.

convenience food | high in fiber | high in salt and sugar | ~~in season~~ | local produce | packaging | processed food | red meat | saturated fat | white meat | whole grains

C Read and complete. Then check (✔) the sentences that are true for you.

1 ◯ I don't really like whole grains, but I know it's good to have plenty of foods that are ________ in my diet.

2 ◯ I like local ________ because I know where it's from and it's better for the environment.

3 ◯ I prefer food that's ________—when you eat food growing now, it tastes better.

4 ◯ We sometimes eat ________ food as it's quick to prepare, but I worry about all the ________ that gets thrown away, and that it's ________ in ________ and ________.

5 ◯ We have some ________ food in our kitchen cabinets, like canned carrots and peas.

6 ◯ I eat more ________, such as chicken, as I don't really like ________, like steak.

7 ◯ My family loves butter, but it contains a lot of ________ so we don't have it often.

D Now listen to the fitness instructor. Why is she talking about diet?

E Listen again. Write *True*, *False*, or *Doesn't Say*.

1 Diet is as important for sports as training. Doesn't Say

2 Changes may be hard but they're worth it. ________

3 A balanced diet includes vitamins and minerals. ________

4 Teenagers especially need more calories. ________

5 We should avoid eating fat. ________

6 Choose water over juice or smoothies. ________

7 It won't take long to notice a difference in how you feel. ________

8 We should eat the same amount of each food group. ________

Why is it important for everyone to have a varied diet?
How do you think our eating habits will change in the future?

A Listen and read. Are Samuel and Uncle Matias talking about food for physical health, for mental health, or for both?

1

2

Samuel: Can I ask your advice, Uncle Matias? I've been studying for my exams but I have a terrible memory.

Uncle Matias: Well, exams are tough. Have you been sleeping well?

Samuel: No, I haven't. I've been waking up a lot at night.

Uncle Matias: Hmm—maybe it's your diet.

Samuel: I guess I haven't been eating healthy food.

Uncle Matias: Well, you know the right kind of food can be good for your brain as well as your body. And what have you been doing to work out?

Samuel: I've been running a lot with my friend—he's been helping me.

Uncle Matias: OK, that's good. Also, think about doing things that will help you sleep, like taking a bath. And make sure any screen time you have is way before bedtime.

Samuel: OK, no phone or tablet before bed.

Uncle Matias: Exactly. Well, I have to go. I'm off to the theater, again.

Samuel: Looks like you haven't been sleeping too much either, Uncle Matias!

B Look at **A**. Complete the table. Where does *not* come in a negative statement?

Present Perfect Progressive

He	______	______	helping	me.
I	______		______	healthy food.

What		______	you	______	doing	to work out?	
______	you	______	______	well?	Yes,	I	have.
					No,		______ .

✔ *He hasn't been revising.*
✘ ~~*He hasn't revising.*~~

Watch Out

C Think and discuss. Then choose.

1 We use the simple past / present perfect progressive to talk about something which started in the past and continues now or which has a present result (cause or effect).

2 We use the present perfect progressive when we want to focus on the duration of the activity / completed action.

D Listen and say.

E Complete with the present perfect progressive. Then write a cause or effect for each sentence.

1 I've been cooking (cook) local produce for the customers in the café all day today.
I'm feeling very hot!

2 You ______ (go) to the gym a lot this week. ______

3 They ______ (not swim) this morning. ______

4 He ______ (eat) more whole grains this month. ______

5 I ______ (not sleep) well this week. ______

6 You look terrible! What have you ______ (do)? ______

7 She ______ (not drink) much water during the day. ______
______

8 We ______ (go to bed) much earlier on weekdays. ______
______

F Play *True or False*. Write and say four sentences about you.

I've been running a lot this week. True or false?

I think that's true.

Yes, it is!

Write About It

A Read the diary entries. What's Luca's problem and his solution?

Monday, June 5

Dear Diary,

This morning, I was running to catch the bus and I felt so sick and out of shape. Also, I've been feeling really tired because I haven't been eating healthily—too much junk food! Ugh! And I've stopped playing sports. Hmm. SO ... I've decided I need to change things. I know it'll make me feel better and I really want to set myself some goals so I can improve. It's hard so I'm going to think about this and write more tomorrow.

Bye for now!

Tuesday, June 6

Hi again,

Today I spoke with some friends about how bad I was feeling. They gave me some great advice. (Thanks, guys!) This is what I've decided to do:

- Eat more healthily—stop eating candy every day and eat snacks low in sugar instead
- Work out—play sports or exercise three times a week
- Be more polite and make sure I'm never late—it's so rude!

I'm going to ask Marek if he wants to do this with me. We could meet up or email each other every Saturday to talk about it and see if we've been doing the things on our list. It'll be way more fun with him and we can encourage each other. I'm going to make it like a competition. Of course, I'm going to win!

Wednesday, June 7

Dear Diary,

YES! First day of new lifestyle for me and Marek! Feeling very excited!

B Look at the structure of the diary entries. Read and answer.

1 Why has Luca included the day and the date for each entry? ____________

2 Put these things in the order Luca writes about them:

a. ☐ why he feels that way c. ☐ how he feels

b. ☐ what he decides to do d. ☐ how he's going to do it

3 Why does he use a list? ____________

4 How do phrases like "Bye for now!", "Hi again!", and "I'm going to ask Marek" help to structure the diary entries? ____________

C Look at the language in the diary entries. Read and respond.

1 Find examples of informal language. Ugh!, ____________

2 Find six descriptions of feelings. ____________

____

D Think and discuss ideas for activities to achieve a better lifestyle. Use one of the Generating Ideas techniques.

E Plan your diary entry. Choose one of your ideas in **D**. Make notes for each question.

1 How do you want to improve yourself?
2 Why is the change important?
3 How do you feel about it?
4 How are you going to do it?

F Now write a diary entry about your plan.

Read and Respond
Read your diary entry again. How do you feel about your plans?

Take the Stage

A Watch and listen. Do you agree with Linda or Veronica?

Watch
Do Linda and Veronica move very much? Why or why not?

B Watch again. Put the information in the order it comes in both speeches.

a. ☐ one reason to support my argument
b. [1] the subject I'm talking about
c. ☐ closing summary
d. ☐ what I believe
e. ☐ other reasons to support my argument

C What do you think? Which argument do you want to support? Think and plan.

Life is more stressful for young people than adults.

For	Against
Young people have to study for exams.	Adults have to go to work.

D Practice with your friends. Then share with the class. Take notes and give feedback.

Did they ...?
- Say which argument they support
- Give reasons
- Give a summary

Reflect
Did I make my reasons clear? Was I persuasive?

How well did you meet the challenge of Unit 2? Read and respond.

My Favorite Mistakes

Means
I
Start
To
Acquire
Knowledge
Experience
Skills

Two mistakes I made in this unit that helped my learning are …

Two things (knowledge) I learned about lifestyles are …

Two things (experience and skills) I learned to say or do in English are …

One thing I want to work on next month is …

This is your goal.

Next month, you'll think about how well your plan worked.

UNIT 1
UNIT 2

Know It, Win It

HOW TO PLAY

1. Play in groups of four. Make counters and choose a color in the center.
2. Use your spinner to move around the board. For each square, answer a question which one of the other players chooses from the Question Sheet printout.

   Computer Cool
   Fun with Food
   Thinking Time
   You've Done It!

3. If you answer correctly, use the spinner to move. If not, try again next turn.
4. If your spinner lands on Open Play, choose a question. Everyone playing the game can answer. The first person to answer correctly has an extra move.
5. Travel once around the board and then go back to the center. Then answer a final Time To Speak question for your color. Talk for one minute to win!

UNIT 3

Dream Big

A Listen. What's different about this theater experience?

- 1 **ambition**
- ☐ **confidence**
- ☐ **determination**
- ☐ **happiness**
- ☐ **health**
- ☐ **pride**
- ☐ **success**
- ☐ **wealth**

B Find and number the words in **A**. Then listen and check.

C Close your eyes. Listen, visualize, and say.

What's your dream?

D Put the words in order of importance for you (1 = most important).

1 ____
2 ____
3 ____
4 ____
5 ____
6 ____
7 ____
8 ____

E Listen and write. Then watch and say.

My Dreams

I have a dream of **1** ambition (mboinita)
I have a lot to do
I'm full of **2** ____ (mettenairiond)
I'm ambitious, through and through!

I have a dream of **3** ____ (cuesssc)
To get right up to the top
I'm full of love and **4** ____ (pishaepsn)
I'm strong, I'll never stop!

I have a dream of **5** ____ (lehawt)
I want to work with **6** ____ (rdipe)
I'm full of energy and **7** ____ (ahhtel)
Live life! Enjoy the ride!

F Pronunciation. Listen and say. Copy the linking. Find other examples in the poem.

have a dream   full of love

A Listen and read. Which doors do Elise and Ji-su choose? Why?

Elise: If you could be anyone, who would you be?

Ji-su: Hmm, if I were someone famous, I'd be a famous athlete—you know, someone with real determination. My sister and I both love sports. She'd be a famous gymnast if she could choose! But if I had the choice, I wouldn't be a gymnast, I'd be a track star because I love running. I'm determined to be a professional track star and go to the Olympics. If I could have anything, I wouldn't have a lot of money, I'd have an Olympic gold medal!

Elise: So, which door are you going to choose?

Ji-su: I can't decide between "Success" and "Pride."

Elise: If I were you, I'd choose "Pride"—imagine how your amazing achievements would make you feel. You would have the satisfaction of going to the Olympics and, who knows, maybe even winning an Olympic medal!

Ji-su: I think I'm going to choose that, too! Let's go!

B Look at **A**. Complete the table. How many times does *would* appear in each sentence?

Second Conditional

If	you	could	______	anyone,	who	______	you be?
______	I	were	someone famous,	I	______	______	a famous athlete.
		______	the choice,		wouldn't		a gymnast.
She	______	be	a gymnast	if	she	______	choose.

She'd be ... = She would be ...

Remember

C Think and discuss. Then choose.

1 We use the second conditional to talk about something which is real or possible / unreal or impossible.

D Listen and say.

E Read and complete the paragraph.

We're all dreamers in my family. If Pietro **1** had (have) the chance, he **2** 'd go (go) to Mars. If I **3** ______ (win) a sports competition, I **4** ______ (be) very proud of myself. When I'm older, I'll have a job, but if I **5** ______ (be) very wealthy, I **6** ______ (not spend) much money—I'd save it. My sister, Elena **7** ______ (not leave) home if she **8** ______ (become) famous, but my parents **9** ______ (move) to Hawaii if they **10** ______ (can) choose.

F Think and discuss. Complete the questions. Then ask and answer.

1 If you had the chance to ______?
2 If you could choose ______?
3 If you found ______?
4 If you were ______?
5 If you won ______?
6 If you didn't have ______?

If you had the chance to learn something new, what would you learn?

If I had the chance, I'd learn to play the piano.

How can children help solve the world's problems?

A Listen to Kamala interviewing three of her teachers. How can adults learn from children?

1 fresh start

2 ____________

3 ____________

4 ____________

5 ____________

6 ____________

7 ____________

8 ____________

B Look at the pictures in **A** and write. Then listen and check.

be the hero	**do things for fun**	**experience failure**	**fear of the unknown**
find joy in	~~**fresh start**~~	**notice the small things**	**nurture friendship**

C Read and complete. Then ask and answer.

1 What things do you find joy in?

2 Do you think of each day as a ______________ start?

3 Do you have a ______________ of the unknown?

4 What things can you do to ______________ friendship?

5 What things do you do for ______________ ?

6 Why is it important to ______________ the small things?

7 How do you feel when you ______________ failure?

8 Do you consider yourself to "be the ______________ of your own story?" Why or why not?

D Now listen to Feliks. How successful were the children in the soccer tournament?

soccer uniform | football kit

E Listen again. Answer the questions.

1 Why was it impossible for the children to play soccer before?

Because they had no space in their village, where all the buildings are over water.

2 What did the adults think of the children's idea at first?

____

____

3 What was the soccer pitch like?

____

4 Why did the adults give the children soccer uniforms?

____

5 How do the adults in the village feel now?

____

What could you do in your community that would benefit young people?
What skills do children need to become positive members of the community?

Explore Language

A Listen and read. How does Juan feel about joining the softball club?

Max: Hi, Juan. Do you want to join the softball club?

Juan: Hi, Max. Yes, but I wish I could play it better. I'm just not very good!

Max: Just play more! Joining a club is a great place to start. My cousin wishes she was better at photography, but she's getting better. She joined a club, and now, she works as a photographer on weekends.

Nella: Everyone has to start somewhere. You know, one of Einstein's teachers didn't think he would do anything with his life, but he kept working hard. And look what he became! I wish I didn't find math so hard, but I just keep trying.

Juan: Yes, but I wish softball wasn't so difficult!

Max: Nella's right. It's all about practice and hard work—but we can help you with that.

Nella: Do you wish you were a great athlete?

Juan: Yes, but …

Max: I wish you'd stop saying "yes, but …" and just join. You won't regret it.

Juan: OK. Yes!

B Look at **A**. Complete the table. What kind of words come after *wish*?

***Wish* + Past Forms**

I	wish	I	______	find	math so hard.
		softball	______		so difficult.
		I	could	______	it better.
		you	______	stop	saying "yes, but ..."
My cousin	______	she	______		better at photography.
______	you	______	you	were	a great athlete?

Watch Out

✔ *I wish I were better at soccer.*

✘ ~~*I wish I am better at soccer.*~~

C Think and discuss. Then choose.

1 We use *I wish I were* ... to talk about a wish which is likely / unlikely to come true.

2 We use *I wish I could* ... to talk about a wish for the ability or permission to do something which is likely / unlikely to come true.

3 We use *I wish you would(n't)* ... to express irritation / happiness.

D Listen and say.

E Find and correct the errors.

1 Do you ~~wished~~ wish you ~~live~~ lived in a different place?

2 I wishes I can help homeless people in my city.

3 I wish I be the hero of the play.

4 Do you wish you have a swimming pool in your town?

5 She wish they'll stop playing their music so loudly.

6 She wish he won't give her so much homework.

F Write three things you wish you could change. Then discuss with a friend.

I wish we could help save animal habitats.

Me, too. Which habitats would you like to help save?

A Read the article. What problems does the lack of electricity cause?

Lighting the Way

What's the problem?

Over a billion people currently live without electricity. In many countries, the power supply is unreliable and expensive. In some places, electricity only comes on once a week. While many cities have access to electricity, many people living in rural areas do not. Although access to electricity is improving, the growing population means that the number of people without access to electricity is increasing.

What does that mean for children?

There are two main effects for schoolchildren. Communication is limited because many people don't have equipment that works properly and they don't have access to the internet. And children without electricity can't study or watch TV after dark. Imagine all of the things that you wouldn't be able to do without electricity!

What's the answer?

The solution lies in finding a reliable, inexpensive source of energy and a way to communicate. Many countries have started using renewable sources of energy, such as solar power and wind power. Some people, including children, are trying to think of new ways to solve the problem themselves in their local communities.

What about the future?

In the future, it is hoped that renewable energy will help solve the lack of electricity. Countries around the world are investing in renewable energy, by building hydroelectric plants, solar farms, and wind farms.

So, what about you? What are you going to do? If you could invent something to help solve the problem, what would it be?

B Look at the structure of the article. Read and respond.

1 What function does the title have?

____

2 Why does the writer use a heading for each paragraph?

____

3 Put the ideas in the order they come in the article.

a. ☐ The future b. ☐ The problem and its cause c. ☐ The solution d. ☐ The effects of the problem

C Look at the language in the article. Complete the Venn Diagram.

limited ~~solution~~ reliable unreliable inexpensive effects difficult problem

Positive	Both	Negative
solution	______	______
______		______
______		______
______		______

Reflect
Using positive and negative adjectives help to clarify the problems, effects, and solutions in a cause and effect article.

Process Writing
Planning, p141

D Think and discuss problems in your local area or region. Complete the mind map.

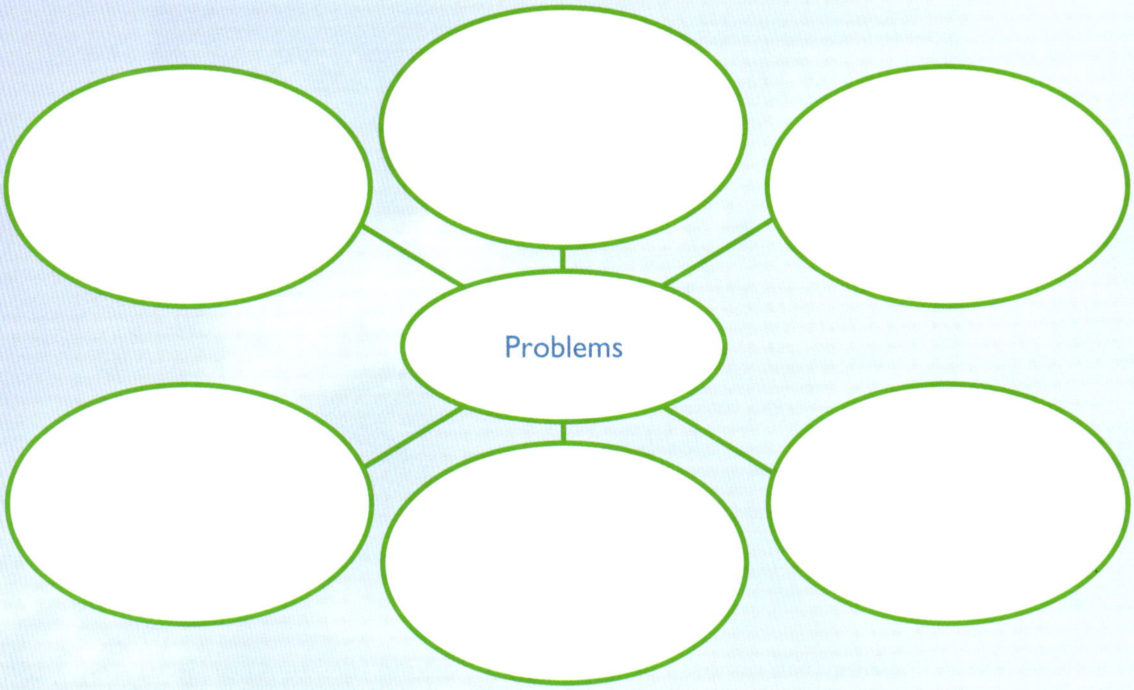

E Plan your article. Choose one of your ideas in **D**. Make notes.

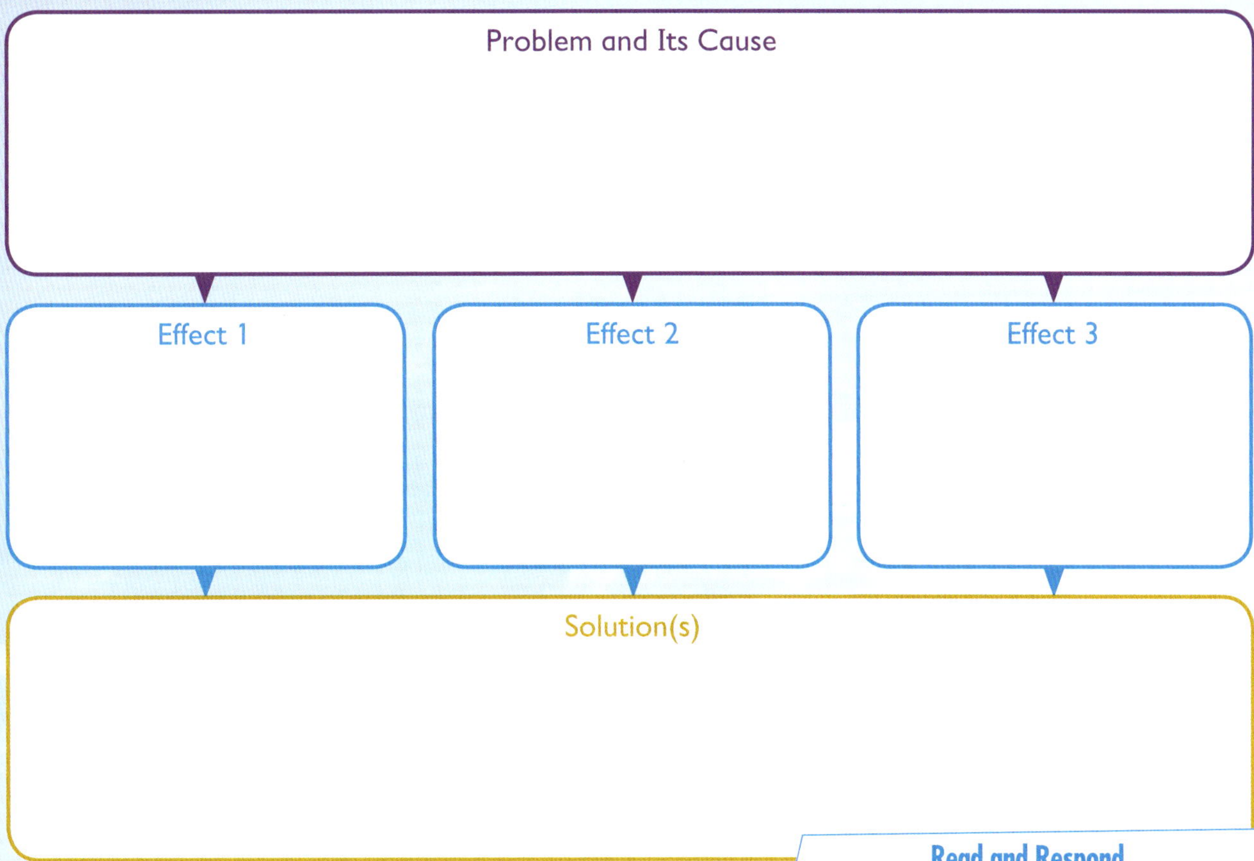

F Now write your article.

Read and Respond
Ask your friend to read your article. Can he/she identify the cause, effects, and solutions to the problem?

A Watch and listen. What ideas are discussed for International Day of Happiness?

Watch
Is Maria sitting down? Why or why not?

B Watch again and number the phrases. Then write *AI* (asking for ideas) or *SU* (summarizing points to ensure understanding).

a. [ ] So, to be clear … ________
b. [1] Can we hear your ideas? AI
c. [ ] You mean we could … ________
d. [ ] Lloyd, what about you? ________
e. [ ] OK, what you're saying is … ________
f. [ ] Linda, what ideas did you have? ________
g. [ ] We could, one, … like … and, two, … like … ________

C Imagine your school is celebrating Universal Children's Day. What ideas do you have?

D Talk with your friends using phrases from **B**. Choose the best three ideas.

organize event | make something | give a performance
invite people | gifts | surprises | other

"We could organize a party."

"I think something permanent might be better. We could plant a tree at the school."

Reflect
Did everyone contribute some ideas to the discussion and understand the outcome?

How well did you meet the challenge of Unit 3? Read and respond.

Monthly Goal Reflection

My goal from Unit 2 was to …

Overall, I rate my effort towards my goal as …

To achieve my goal I …

Other things I learned or improved this month …

Next month

I will continue to work on this goal. I will set myself a new goal.

My plan now is to …

Hello! Remember me? I'm Max and I like softball, photography, and astronomy. Do you know what ball lightning is? Find out in Unit 4!

UNIT 4

How's That Possible?

A Listen. What mystery are Sachin and his friends discussing?

- 1 evidence
- fact
- have a feeling
- make up
- optical illusion
- play a trick
- puzzle
- see things

B Find and number the words in A. Then listen and check.

C Close your eyes. Listen, visualize, and say.

D Look and write.

1 solve a puzzle
2 find ________
3 see an ________
4 explain a ________
5 have a ________
6 make ________
7 see ________
8 play a ________

E Listen and write. Then watch and say.

My Friend Oscar

Well, my friend Oscar, just for kicks,
Likes to play a lot of 1 tricks .
He likes to cause great confusion
By setting up an 2 o________ i________ .

Let me tell you I have a 3 f________
He finds mysteries very appealing.
He tells us 4 "f________ ," but then we see
He's just 5 m________ them up, entirely.

He makes us think we're 6 s________ t________ ,
He spends hours and hours preparing things.
But really the only great big 7 p________
Is why Oscar goes to all this trouble.

F Pronunciation. Listen and say. Copy the linking. Find other examples of linking in the poem.

jus(t) for kicks   grea(t) confusion   le(t) me tell you

Explore Language

A Listen and read. What do all the photos have in common?

1

2

Jenna: Look at this photo. It's weird, isn't it? Her feet look really big!

Max: It's an optical illusion, Jenna! They must have put the shoes by the camera, then the photographer must have lain down on the ground.

Noor: Hmm. This one with two people is a bit of a puzzle. They might have put two photographs together.

Jenna: But they're in the same room, Noor. Could they have done it with a computer, do you think? That's cheating!

Max: They must have used Photoshop because the person on the right is really big!

Noor: Oh look, in this one it looks like his head's a flower pot!

Max: No—look. He pulled his sweater over his head then sat in front of the pot. But you can still see his hair. They can't have spent very long on that one!

Noor: Oh, I want to try it! Come on, let's take some trick photos!

B Look at **A**. Complete the table. How many verbs are in this structure?

Modals of Deduction: Past Forms

They	must	have	________	the shoes by the camera.
	may/________			two photographs together.
	________	________	spent	very long on that one!
________	they	have	________	it with a computer?

C Think and discuss. Then choose and write.

✔ *She must have taken it.*
✘ *~~She must of taken it.~~*
Watch Out

1 We use past modals of deduction / obligation to talk about how sure we are that something is true about a past action or event.

2 very sure it's true — quite sure it's true — possibly true — sure it isn't true

________ may have ________ ________

D Listen and say.

E Complete the dialogue with the correct form of the verbs.

Stella: Oh no! I've lost my camera!

Kai: 1 Could you have left (leave) it in the gym? You left in a rush.

Stella: Oh, it's OK, it's here. But the photos are all deleted!

Kai: Hold on, you 2 ________ (not lose) them. Let me look … Don't worry, they're there.

Stella: Wait up … where's Marco? His bag isn't here, so he 3 ________ (go) home.

Kai: Yes, but he left these photos. I'm sure he won't mind if we have a look. When did he take this one?

Stella: He 4 ________ (take) it last night. There wasn't a full moon.

Kai: Look at how small that person is.

Stella: Yes, they 5 ________ (be) a long way away.

Kai: Do you think he used a trick in this photo?

Stella: He 6 ________ (do) that, but I'm not sure. It's really good!

F Think and discuss. Look at some pictures in this book or in magazines. What deductions can you make?

Look on p. 40. These children must have been friends for a long time.

Yes, they might have met at school.

Why is it important to explore things we don't understand?

A Listen to Fairuza and Theo watch a TV documentary about Stonehenge. Why is Stonehenge a mystery?

1 prehistoric times

2 ____________

3 ____________

4 ____________

5 ____________

6 ____________

an idea to explain how or why something happens

7 ____________

8 ____________

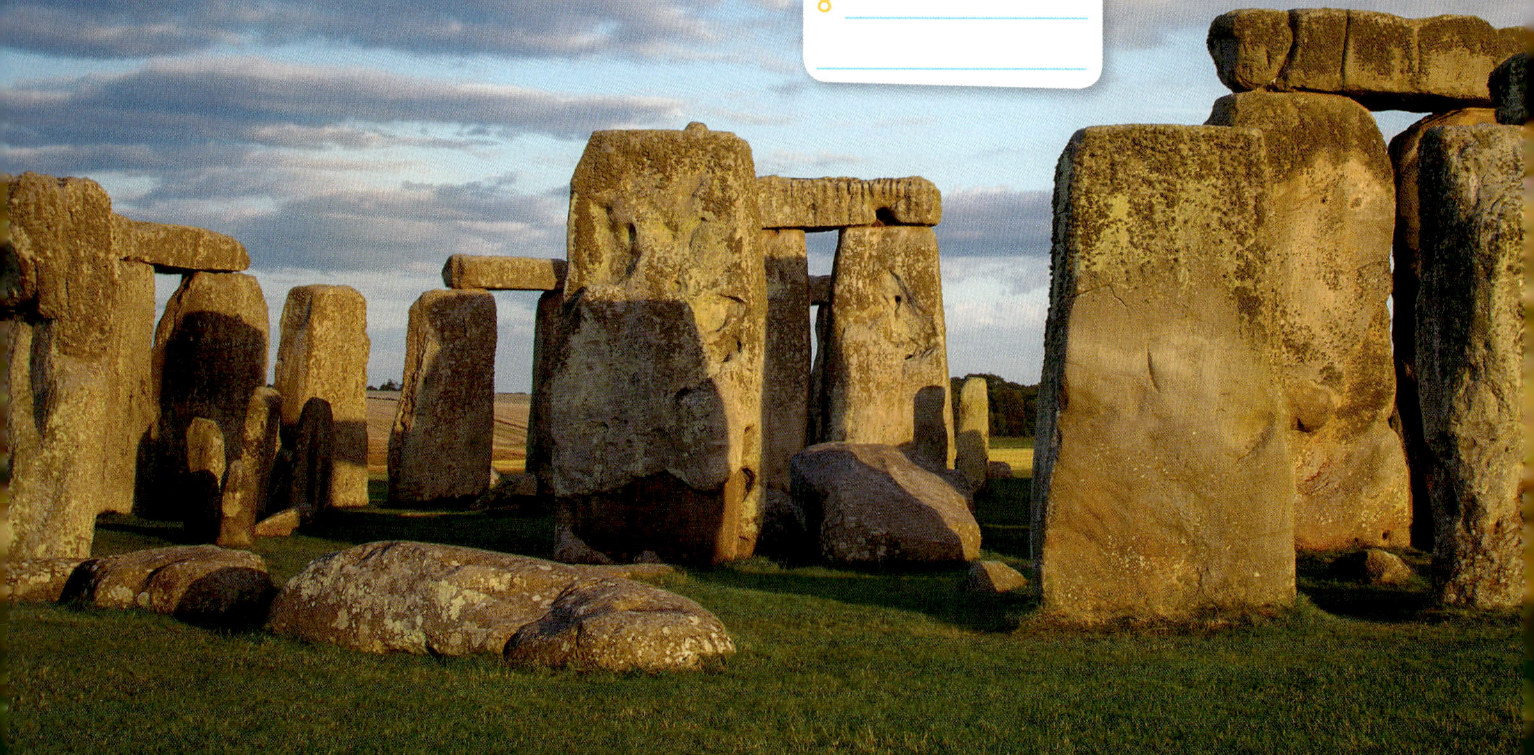

B Look at the pictures and definition in **A** and write. Then listen and check.

ancient monument   archaeologist   clue   expert
legend   ~~prehistoric times~~   solve   theory

C Read. Write the words for the underlined part of the sentences.

1 Stonehenge is a very old site which is preserved for people to look at. It's the most famous one in Britain. ancient monument

2 I have an explanation of how the Great Pyramid of Giza was built. ________

3 We finally managed to find an answer to the mystery. ________

4 Some people lived in caves during the period in history before writing. ________

5 We don't know which old story of those told about Pocahontas is really true. ________

6 I love being the person who looks at the remains of buildings to learn about people and society on this project. ________

7 He's an extremely knowledgeable person about the history of Peru. He knows everything! ________

8 This is a very important piece of information which will help us find the solution to the problem. ________

D Now listen to Fairuza's classmate Yasin. Which site is his presentation about? Do experts know all the facts about this place?

E Listen again. Read and choose.

1 We can learn a lot about today's society from legends / ancient history.

2 Some think the underwater city was built hundreds / thousands of years ago.

3 The ruins cover a very large / small area.

4 Scientists agree / disagree about how the city was created.

5 One big structure is the shape of a rectangle / pyramid.

6 Some people think the city became buried because of a natural disaster / an explosion.

What mysteries surround different historical sites in your country? What problems are causing damage to the world's cultural sites? Are there any solutions?

Explore Language

A Listen and read. What do you think the children see in the park?

1

Inez: Mrs. Lewis! We just saw the Yeti or Bigfoot in the woods!

Mrs. Lewis: Are you sure, Inez? There isn't any evidence that they exist. Is someone just playing a trick?

2

Kayla: No, it's true! We didn't have to stay late at school, so we went to the park. We wanted to take some photos for our club competition. Then we heard a strange noise coming from a group of trees.
We went nearer and saw a dark shape. We had to get pretty close to see it better.

3

Mrs. Lewis: You shouldn't have gotten too near, Kayla. Weren't you scared?!

Inez: We wanted to solve the mystery.

Mrs. Lewis: Well, what did it look like? You should have taken some photos as evidence for your theory!

Kayla: We tried to take a photo—but then suddenly it disappeared!

B Look at **A**. Complete the table. What's the opposite of *had to*?

Modals of Obligation: Past Forms

We	______ to		get	pretty close.
	didn't ______ to		______	late at school.
You	______	______	taken	some photos.
	shouldn't	______	______	too near.

Watch Out

✔ *I had to solve the mystery yesterday.*
✘ ~~*I must solve the mystery yesterday.*~~

C Think and discuss. Then choose.

1 We use *had to* to say something was / wasn't necessary in the past and *didn't have to* to say something was / wasn't necessary in the past.

2 We use *should've* and *shouldn't have* to say we wish we could change something in the past / future.

D Listen and say.

E Complete the email with the correct form of the verbs.

Hi Doctor Picture Fix,

For our club last week we 1 had to choose (choose) something to photograph. It was great because we 2 ______ (do) anything specific—it was a free choice. But we 3 ______ (find) something that could be interpreted in different ways. I chose a group of trees but I 4 ______ (choose) that because there was a problem. When I got home, I saw something that looked like a strange animal in the photo! Now my friends are saying it's a trick photo but it's real. I 5 ______ (take) more photos. How can I show that the photo isn't fake?

From Giulio

F Think of a project you had to do for school. What did/didn't you have to do? Make notes then talk with a friend. Give each other advice.

– Had to do a project on a mystery
– Didn't have to make a model
– Had to do research–hard because I didn't have time

Last week I had to do a project on Bigfoot.

Oh! You should have told me! I know a lot about Bigfoot.

Write About It

A Read the beginning of a story. What do we learn about the Russian Guide?

OUR RUSSIAN GUIDE

My sister, Talia, and I had a really strange experience when we were on vacation in Russia last year. We went to Moscow in the winter. It was amazing: bitterly cold and icy. Talia and I didn't really know much about Russia before we went but we learned a lot in a totally unexpected way.

The first morning, my parents went to the bank. Talia and I stayed in the hotel café checking a map of the city. We were getting bored when a boy came over to us. He must have been the same age as us. He was tall with blond hair. He said, "I heard you talking about Russia. It's sad you don't know anything." We were surprised but he sat down and started pointing to places on our map. Then he told us about every important place in Moscow. We were completely absorbed because he told us fascinating stories about each place.

Suddenly he said, "I must go." He stood up quickly and went without saying goodbye.

When our parents came back, we told them about the boy. My dad went to the waiter to ask about him so he could meet him and say thank you. But the waiter said he hadn't noticed anyone else in the café that morning. That's when our adventure started: we had to solve the mystery of our Russian guide.

B Look at the structure of the beginning of the story. Check (✔) the information you need to include. Say why.

1 (✔) The place ____________

2 ( ) The solution ____________

3 ( ) The main characters ____________

4 ( ) The reason the characters are in the place ____________

____

5 ( ) The relationship between the main characters ____________

____

6 ( ) How the characters change or grow ____________

7 ( ) What the place looked or felt like ____________

8 ( ) A problem ____________

C Look at the language in the beginning of the story. Read and answer.

1 Find examples of time phrases. Why are they important? last year, ____________

____

2 Underline examples of adjectives showing feelings and reactions. Why are they important?

____

D Think and discuss. Choose a vacation, cultural visit, or weekend outing for your story. Brainstorm some ideas using one of the Generating Ideas techniques.

Scene/Setting	Characters	Problem/Mystery

E Plan the beginning of your story. Look at your ideas in **D**. Make notes. Then order the events.

☐ Idea ______________________

____

Time phrase ______________________

Adjectives ______________________

☐ Idea ______________________

____

Time phrase ______________________

Adjectives ______________________

☐ Idea ______________________

____

Time phrase ______________________

Adjectives ______________________

☐ Idea ______________________

____

Time phrase ______________________

Adjectives ______________________

Read and Respond
Ask your friend to read your story. What does he/she think might happen next?

F Now write the beginning of your story.

Take the Stage

A Watch and listen. What would you most like to know about the statues?

Watch
When do Veronica and Lloyd use hand gestures? Why?

B Watch again. Read and respond. Then discuss.

1 Check (✔) the questions you hear.

a. ✔ Do you know about the statues …?

b. ◯ Where did they come from?

c. ◯ Have you ever thought about this?

d. ◯ What do you think?

2 Why does the first speaker use questions? ______

3 Why does she use pauses? ______

4 Does the second speaker ask questions? Why or why not? ______

______

C Think of a cultural place would you like to talk about. Think and plan. Then write notes for your presentation.

Place I've chosen	
Reasons why	
Interesting facts	
Questions to ask audience	

Reflect
Which was the best question I asked to get the audience thinking?

D Practice with your friends. Then share with the class. Take notes and give feedback.

How well did you meet the challenge of Unit 4? Read and respond.

3 · 2 · 1

3 things I learned in this unit

1 ______________________

2 ______________________

3 ______________________

2 "Ah-ha!" moments I had

1 ______________________

2 ______________________

An "ah-ha!" moment is when you suddenly realize you understand something.

1 big question I still have

____

Hello! Remember me? I'm Mrs. Lewis. I really enjoy photography, but I teach a different subject. What do you think I teach my students? Find out in Unit 5!

UNIT 3

UNIT 4

Chatter

GOOD QUALITIES

MY DREAMS

- What kind of things do you find joy in?
- What's the expression for when you start something again?
- What's the opposite of being the villain?

IF ONLY

THAT'S STRANGE

- What's the opposite of fiction?
- What's the phrase for something that looks very different from what it really is?
- Tell me about a trick you shouldn't have played on someone.

HOW TO PLAY

Student A

1 Play in pairs.

2 Choose a green picture box and say the title. Student B asks a question, which you must answer. He/She awards you points for your answer: 2 = excellent/correct answer; 1 = good answer; 0 = poor/incorrect answer. Log the points on your chart.

3 Now Student B chooses a title and you ask one of the questions from the blue question boxes. Award points for the answer. Discuss with your friend if you disagree.

4 Take turns until all the questions have been answered. The student with the most points wins!

______'s Points

LIFE MIGHT BE DIFFERENT

- Where would you go if you could travel anywhere?
- If you could visit an ancient site, what would you like to see?
- If you were a hero, who would you be?

FASCINATING HISTORY

OBLIGATIONS

- What did you have to do in the past that you don't do now?
- Is there anything you should have done yesterday that you didn't do? What?
- Think of a time when you did something didn't have to. What did you do? Why did you do it?

I WONDER

Boxes

LIFE MIGHT BE DIFFERENT

FASCINATING HISTORY

- Give me an example of an ancient monument.
- What's the word for something you see or find that helps you solve a mystery?
- What is the period of very early history called?

OBLIGATIONS

I WONDER

- Tell me about a time when a result could have been different.
- How do you think people might have built Stonehenge?
- What do you think may have happened to cities under water?

HOW TO PLAY

Student B

1 Play in pairs.

2 Student A chooses a title and you ask one of the questions from the green question boxes. Award points for the answer: 2 = excellent/correct answer; 1 = good answer; 0 = poor/incorrect answer. Discuss with your friend if you disagree.

3 Now you choose a blue picture box and say the title. Student A asks a question, which you must answer. He/She awards you points. Log the points on your chart.

4 Take turns until all the questions have been answered. The student with the most points wins!

__________'s Points

GOOD QUALITIES

- Tell me about an ambition you have.
- What is the word for when you feel very sure of success?
- What's the opposite of poverty when you're describing a country?

MY DREAMS

IF ONLY

- Tell me three things you wish for and why.
- What do you wish hadn't happened?
- Which period of history do you wish you had lived in? Why?

THAT'S STRANGE

UNIT 5

What Is Art?

A Listen. Which two paintings does Tyler like? Why?

- [ ] abstract shapes
- [ ] complex
- 1 doodles
- [ ] dots
- [ ] lines
- [ ] playful
- [ ] powerful
- [ ] serious
- [ ] simple
- [ ] squiggles

B Find and number the words in **A**. Then listen and check.

C Close your eyes. Listen, visualize, and say.

D Look and write.

Things you can see in a painting:

1 dots 3 ________ 5 ________

2 ________ 4 ________ ________

Ways of describing a painting:

6 ________ 8 ________ 10 ________

7 ________ 9 ________

E **Listen and write. Then watch and say.**

The More I Look

A Poem Inspired by Kandinsky

I can see colors—bright and clear.
The more I look, the more they appear.
Red 1 dots dance before my eyes,
An 2 a________ shape? A black bird flies.

I can see 3 s________ —messy and free.
The more I look, the more I see.
A 4 s________ face with a 5 p________ stare.
6 D________ of dogs. And a big yellow square.

I can see 7 l________ —in front and behind.
The more I look, the more I find.
A 8 p________ painting. What does it mean?
I'm not sure. But I like the green.

F **Pronunciation. Listen and say. Copy the sentence stress. Think of other sentences like these.**

The more I look, the more they appear.

The more I look, the more I see.

Explore Language

A Listen and read. How did Kofi's paintings change when he came back from Paris?

Mrs. Lewis: Hi, Kofi!

Kofi: Hey, Mom, thanks again for taking me to Paris! Before we went there, I hadn't realized it was so cool!

Mrs. Lewis: I know, it's great, isn't it?

Kofi: I loved those amazing paintings in the street. I'd never seen anything like them before.

Mrs. Lewis: Yes, they were beautiful and so realistic, weren't they? Had you heard of the artist, Patrick Commecy, before we went to Paris?

Kofi: No, I'd read about a lot of artists in the Louvre art gallery but I hadn't heard about that street artist before. I'd already been thinking about different ways of painting and he's really inspired me to make my paintings bigger.

Mrs. Lewis: Oh, really?

Kofi: Yes, I'd never thought about art in that way before. Come and see what I've done!

Mrs. Lewis: What? Where are we going?

Kofi: I want to show you something in the yard. Here! Look! Ta-da!

Mrs. Lewis: Oh, wow! That's amazing! I love it!

B Look at **A**. Complete the table. What's the difference between the simple and progressive forms?

Past Perfect and Past Perfect Progressive

I	______	______			about a lot of artists.
		never	______		anything like them before.
I	______	already	been	______	about different ways of painting.
______	you	heard			of the artist before we went to Paris?

Watch Out

✔ *I'd been thinking about it.*
✘ ~~*I been thinking about it.*~~

C Think and discuss. Then choose.

1 We use the past perfect to talk about an action completed in the past before / after another action was completed.

2 We use the past perfect / past perfect progressive to focus on the finished action.

3 The past perfect / past perfect progressive talks about an activity in progress in the past.

D Listen and say.

E Write full sentences using the correct form of the underlined verbs.

1 Before I / start / adding doodles, I / not realize / drawing was so fun.

Before I started adding doodles, I hadn't realized drawing was so fun.

2 He / never want / to go to an art gallery before his uncle / take / him.

______

3 I / not hear / of Commecy until my mother / tell / me about him.

______

4 She / draw / for years before she / start / painting as well.

______

5 They / look / at paintings for hours when they / realize / the gallery was about to close.

______

F Imagine you're in these situations. How did you get into them? Talk to your friend.

Sitting in the yard with my face painted blue.

Running after my pet rabbit in the mall.

Dressed as a donut and walking to school.

I'd been painting my tree house ...

What can art tell us about different countries and periods of time?

A Listen to Eugene ask Felicity about the Statue of Liberty. Do they think the Statue of Liberty is a work of art?

1 symbolize

2 ____________

3 ____________

4 ____________

the way that someone produces art or music, or writes

5 ____________

the ability to create new ideas or things using your imagination

6 ____________

7 ____________

describe someone or something using words or pictures

8 ____________

B Look at the pictures and definitions in **A** and write. Then listen and check.

contrast creativity depict iconic large-scale masterpiece style ~~symbolize~~

C Read and complete. Then ask and answer.

1 What piece of art do you think is a masterpiece ? Why?

2 Do you prefer paintings that ______ people or places?

3 Can you think of an ______ building in your country?

4 Do you like an abstract ______ of painting or something more realistic?

5 What do you think a white bird often ______ in art?

6 Do you like ______ art or something much smaller?

7 Do you like paintings that have a big ______ in colors or something simpler?

8 In what area is your country more famous for its ______ : art or music?

D Now listen to Bo, the art gallery guide. How were kites used in the past?

E Listen again. Answer the questions.

1 Why is the painting important to Bo? Because his parents and grandparents used to play with kites.

2 When were kites invented? ______

3 What is the legend of the first kite? ______

4 In which countries was kite-flying popular? ______

5 When did kites become popular as toys? ______

6 What started in the 1900s? ______

7 What does Bo think about the dragon kites? ______

What objects do you think best represent your country?
In what ways does art benefit individuals and communities?

Explore Language

A Listen and read. Describe Aaliyah's self-portrait.

Aaliyah: I'm going to enter the Art Club portrait competition with this selfie.

Hugo: A selfie? Is that allowed?

Aaliyah: Yes, I think it's an interesting way of doing a portrait. Isn't a selfie just a modern self-portrait? While I was looking at some old paintings, I was thinking about how things are now. In the past, artists painted self-portraits because they didn't have cameras. They often included objects in their paintings to show details about their lives. I decided to take a selfie and also include something I like doing. So, I took a photo of me playing chess. What were you thinking of doing?

Hugo: I was wondering about it this morning and I'd decided to take a photograph. But now I'm going to do a traditional painting. I'd been thinking of doing a self-portrait but I'd rather do someone else. Maybe I could paint a portrait of you and your selfie. So there's art inside art!

B Look at **A**. Complete the table. How many verbs does each narrative tense have?

Narrative Tenses

Simple Past	In the past, artists	painted			self-portraits.
Past Progressive	I	_____	_____		about how things are now.
Past Perfect	I	_____	_____		to take a photograph.
Past Perfect Progressive			_____	_____	of doing a self-portrait.

You can use more than one narrative tense in one sentence.

Look

C Think and discuss. Then choose.

1 We use the four narrative tenses to talk about the past / present.

2 We use narrative tenses in instructions / stories and personal anecdotes to describe events and situations.

3 We can use conjunctions, linking words, and time phrases (*but*, *while*, *but now*) to show the sequence / importance of events in a narrative.

D Listen and say.

E Read the anecdote and choose. Then underline the time phrases and connecting words.

While we were biking to the exhibition, we **1** were seeing / saw something strange. I **2** was deciding / decided to take a photo. While I **3** was setting up / had set up the selfie, I dropped my phone. I **4** was leaning / leaned over to get it when a cow mooed loudly behind me. I **5** was forgetting / 'd forgotten we were in a field of cows, so I jumped with fright. As I was falling, I managed to take a selfie of me and the cow! Before that, I **6** hadn't been planning / didn't plan to enter the portrait competition, but I think I will now.

leaned

leant

F Play a chain game. Think of a situation to start the game. Then say what happened next.

I was cleaning up my room when the picture fell off the wall.

I was cleaning up my room when the picture fell off the wall! I was picking the picture up when the alarm went off.

Write About It

A Look at the picture. What kind of story does it make you think of? Read. Which of the three mini sagas is most like your idea?

A On my birthday, Uncle Jim took me out in his boat—an exciting experience I'd been waiting for! But the calm sea quickly became stormy and the boat's motor stopped. This wasn't the adventure we'd planned. Terrified, I held tightly onto the boat until we finally returned to the beach.

B As I waited for my father's blue fishing boat, I could only think about dinner. I was so hungry I could have eaten all night. They pulled the boat onto the beach and I hoped to see hundreds of silver fish. I couldn't believe my eyes when I saw just one!

C Peter was walking on the beach as usual and he had a feeling something incredible would happen that day. So far, he'd only found useless things: torn nets, one shoe. Then, amazingly, he spotted a message in a bottle at the bottom of a boat that would change his life.

A mini saga is a piece of writing which has exactly 50 words.

B Look at the structure of the mini sagas. Read and answer.

1 Are these sentences from the beginning, middle, or end of mini saga A?

a. the adventure we'd planned ______

b. an exciting experience ______

c. quickly became stormy / motor stopped ______

2 Look at the underlined phrases in mini saga B. How are they connected? What effect do they have on the reader? ______

3 Which phrases in mini saga C create similar links to those in B? ______

C Look at the language in the mini sagas. Copy and complete the table.

Mini saga	Sights and sounds	Emotions and feelings	Time (past and future)
A			
B	blue fishing boat / hundreds of silver fish / just one	think about dinner / hungry / couldn't believe my eyes	all night
C			

Good writing is about the choices of words, not how much you write.

D Think and discuss. Choose a painting you like for a mini saga. Brainstorm lots of ideas for each of the headings using a Generating Ideas technique.

What you see and hear | Emotions and feelings | Time (past and future)

E Plan your mini saga. Use some of your ideas in **D** and one of the Planning techniques.

F Now write your mini saga in 50 words. Give your mini saga a title.

Read and Respond
Ask your friend to read your mini saga. Can he/she identify a beginning, middle, and end which link together?

A Watch and listen. What are the three points Gene wants to emphasize in his speech?

Watch
Where does Gene look most: at his notes or at the audience?

B Watch again. Put the phrases in the order you hear them.

a. ☐ So, to repeat: …
b. 1 Ladies and gentlemen, boys and girls …
c. ☐ We're very pleased to see …
d. ☐ Welcome to …
e. ☐ Thank you for coming …
f. ☐ We're really proud to …
g. ☐ I'd like to point out three things: one, … two, … and three, …

C You're going to make the welcome speech for an event at your school. Think and plan.

Event name:

Event theme and reasons:

Special feature of the event:

Particular emphasis for this year's event:

People involved in the event:

My favorite part of the event:

D Practice with your friends. Then share with the class. Take notes and give feedback.

Reflect
Did I summarize my points?

How well did you meet the challenge of Unit 5? Read and respond.

Looking Back

My favorite activity was …

One thing I learned is …

The funniest moment this month was when …

I'll never forget when …

UNIT 6

It's Your Turn

A Listen. Which game is Simon most interested in playing: chess, *Go*, or backgammon? Why?

- [ ] **board game**
- [ ] **chance**
- [ ] **land on**
- [ ] **lose**
- [ ] **miss a turn**
- [ ] **pieces**
- [ ] **players**
- 1 **strategy**
- [ ] **throw the dice**
- [ ] **win**

6 way things happen without being planned or expected

B Find and number the words in **A**. Then listen and check.

C Close your eyes. Listen, visualize, and say.

D Complete the crossword.

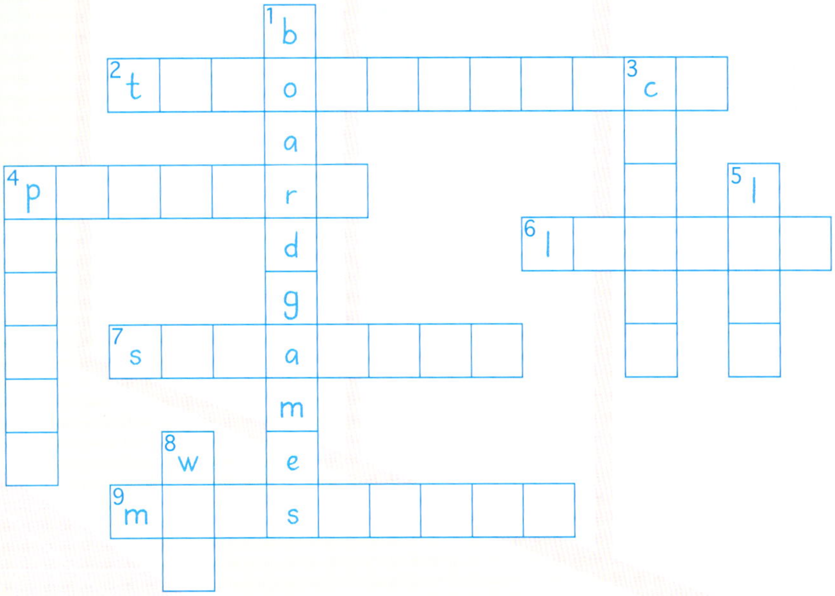

E Listen and write. Then watch and say.

Fun and Games

A game of 1 chance (nechac). Which is my square?
I take my turn. Don't 2 ________ (danl) on there!
I move my piece. I count to eight.
I move again. Oh, that's great!

My 3 ________ (nurt) again. I'll move on now.
I have two twos. I don't know how.
I move my piece. I count to four.
I 4 ________ (smis) a turn. Oh, are you sure?

I take my piece. I throw the 5 ________ (edic).
I got a five. I got it twice.
I move my 6 ________ (iepec). I count to ten.
I miss a turn. Oh, not again!

Win or 7 ________ (osel), it's fun to play.
Another game? Well, yeah, OK!

F Pronunciation. Listen and say. Copy the intonation. Think of other phrases like these.

Oh, that's great! Oh, not again!

A Listen and read. What activities are Simon and Marge doing?

1

Simon: Great! I can do my puzzles in peace and quiet.

Marge: I'm going to play a word game! Do you know how to play, Simon?

Simon: No, I don't.

2

Marge: I have to find two opposites for each word. Can you tell me what the opposites of "light" are?

Simon: Dark. Heavy.

Marge: Yes! And I wonder whether you know the two opposites of "lost."

Simon: Found. Won.

Marge: Oh, you're good at this! I wonder if you can answer this one.

3

Simon: Marge, I'm trying to do my puzzle.

Marge: Yes, but I'm not sure what the two opposites of "right" are …

Simon: That's easy, but what about this one? Do you have any idea what the opposite of "noisy" is?

Marge: Yes, it's "quiet!" Oh, you mean *me* … ha, ha!

B Look at **A**. Complete the table. Is the word order after the *wh–* word like a statement or a question?

Indirect questions

I		wonder	________	you	know	the two opposites of "lost."
			________		can answer	this one.
I	'm	not sure	________	the two opposites of right ________ .		
Can		you	________	me	________	the opposites of light are?

C Think and discuss. Then choose.

1 Indirect questions are less polite than direct questions. True / False

I wonder if/whether you can help me.

Remember

D Listen and say.

E Read and write the indirect questions.

1 Do you like playing card games?

I wonder if you like playing card games .

2 Which is the most popular board game?

Do you have any idea ________________________________ ?

3 When did you last do a puzzle from a book?

Do you know ________________________________ ?

4 Have you ever played a board game online?

I'm not sure ________________________________ .

5 Would you like to invent a board game?

Can you tell me ________________________________ ?

F Interview your friend. Follow the instructions. Then ask and answer.

1 Each person chooses to be someone famous that you like.
2 Interview each other as the famous person. Use indirect questions.
3 Ask about free time activities, including any games the famous person plays.

Can you tell me which your favorite board game is? Why?

I wonder how often you play it.

How can games help you learn about other ways of life?

A Listen to Kendra help her brother Malik to choose an online game. Can you describe the game?

1 avatar

2 ________

3 ________

4 ________

5 ________

6 ________

for more than one player in the same game at the same time

7 ________

work with someone in order to produce something

8 ________

gain enough points in a game to improve your avatar

9 ________

a game in which you pretend to be someone else, especially in order to learn new skills or attitudes

10 ________

B B Look at the pictures and definitions in **A** and write. Then listen and check.

~~avatar~~	collaborate	collect points	gaming	graphics
instructions	level up	multiplayer	role-playing game	virtual

C Read and complete.

1 I've collected enough points to level up so I'll gain more skills for my character.

2 Many teachers now recognize the educational benefits of __________ .

3 We tried to follow the __________ , but they weren't very clear.

4 Your __________ can talk to others and the words appear in a speech bubble.

5 They've created a realistic __________ world in the new role-playing game.

6 I wonder whether it's a _______________ game or whether I have to play it on my own.

7 My sister's taking a course in computer __________ .

8 What I like best about this game is that you're all part of a community and __________ .

D Now listen to Mr. Suvlu, an Inupiat teacher from Alaska. What's special about this game?

E Listen again. Read and match the sentence halves.

1 The teacher wants the students to use the game (f)

2 The game is based on

3 Players can only progress if they can

4 The game allows players

5 The game is interesting because it

6 Players can learn about

a. stop the weather causing problems.

b. has videos from real people.

c. to visit the Alaskan Arctic in a virtual world.

d. stories that the Inupiat people tell.

e. why the stars are important to the Inupiat people.

f. to find out about another culture.

What challenges do you have in your studies that games might help address? What other skills and life skills can we learn from playing games?

A Listen and read. What does a team have to do to win *The Name in the Hat* game?

1 Get into two teams.

2 Each team member writes down the name of a famous person on a piece of paper. It must be someone who you all know.

3 Fold all the pieces of paper up and put them in a hat, which you put in front of everyone.

4 A member from each team takes turns to take a piece of paper out of the hat. The player whose name has the most letters starts first.

5 Each team member has one minute to try to help *their* team guess the name. You can use mime or say something about the person, like "He lives in the place where a lot of actors live," but you *can't* say the name.

6 The other team has to try to guess the name first.

7 The team that guesses the most names correctly, wins!

B Look at **A**. Complete the table. Which sentence has a comma before the relative pronoun?

Defining and Non-defining Relative Clauses

It must be someone	who/that	you all know.
The player	______	name has the most letters starts first.
"He lives in the place	______	a lot of actors live."
Put them in a hat,	______	you put in front of everyone.

It's the game that ~~it~~ involves miming.

Watch Out

C Think and discuss. Then choose.

1 We can use defining and non-defining relative clauses to give more information about the subject / object / subject and/or object.

2 We use defining / non-defining relative clauses to give extra, non-essential information.

3 We usually use *that* in sentences with relative clauses when we're speaking. True / False

D Listen and say.

E Complete the anecdote. Use a relative pronoun and one of the relative clauses in the box.

> **she needed to dress up for** **bedroom door was open**
> **was sitting on the bed. But it was only her sister playing a trick** **was exciting**
> ~~**enjoyed playing games with her friends**~~

1 Hannah was a young girl who enjoyed playing games with her friends.

2 She had a new role-playing game ______.

3 The game was about superheroes, ______.

4 Hannah decided to borrow a costume from her sister, ______.

5 As she walked into her sister's bedroom, she saw a monster, ______ ______!

F Read and complete the sentences about yourself. Then talk with a friend.

A talent which I would like to have is being able to sing.

What would you like to sing?

1 A time when ...
2 A place ...
3 A person ...
4 A talent ...

Write About It

A **Read the article. Which type of games does the writer prefer? Why?**

www.lettheparentstalk.com

Old, New, Which Game Is for You?

Which kind of games do you prefer to play? Most of my friends enjoy playing modern video games. But, for a super fun time, I prefer traditional games. Let me tell you why.

I do play video games and it is exciting when you have to follow an adventure and you win something in the end. I also like games where you can level up a character. Not only are these games really engaging, but they also look great: the design is technically brilliant and the graphics can be incredibly realistic. So, it's easy to see how you can spend so much time playing them. But I feel that I waste hours of time just playing by myself and there's no one to share the excitement with. Even if the game is multiplayer, you're usually still alone in the room.

Traditional but not boring

Traditional games can be just as engaging and, in role-playing board games for example, you can be fantastically imaginative. But the big difference is that if you play a simple board game, you can talk to the other players in person, which I really enjoy. And the challenges in games like chess are great for your brain, although they're extremely difficult!

All in all, I prefer traditional games because, although they may feel "old school" in comparison to the new video games available, to me they're way more fun, as you can spend quality time with your friends. Try and you'll see!

Video game fun

B **Look at the structure of the article. Check (✔) what information is included. Then put the information in order.**

a. ◯ ☐ Reasons why the first type of game is good

b. ◯ ☐ Games his children like

c. ◯ ☐ A comparison

d. ✔ 1 An introduction question

e. ◯ ☐ Reasons why the second type of game is good

f. ◯ ☐ Why the writer is writing the article

g. ◯ ☐ A summarizing comment

C **Look at the language in the article. Read and match the collocations.**

1 super fun
2 technically brilliant
3 incredibly realistic
4 fantastically imaginative
5 extremely difficult

a. graphics
b. design
c. role-playing board games
d. challenges
e. time

D Think and discuss. Choose two kinds of games you've played. Complete the mind map with your ideas.

Process Writing
Drafting, p142

Game 1

Name ______

Reasons game is good ______

______

______

Adjectives ______

Game 2

Name ______

Reasons game is good ______

______

______

Adjectives ______

My comparisons

______

______

______

E Plan your article. Use your ideas in **D** and one of the Planning techniques. Make notes for each paragraph.

Title: ______

Paragraph 1: ______

______

Paragraph 2: ______

______

Paragraph 3: ______

______

Paragraph 4: ______

______

F Write a first draft for your article. Read it and decide how you can improve it.

G Now write your article.

Read and Respond
Ask your friend to read your article. Which of the two kinds of games does he/she prefer?

Talk About It

A Watch and listen. What do Veronica and Linda decide to do?

Watch
How do Veronica and Linda show how they're listening to each other's points?

B Watch again. Check (✔) the phrases you hear. Write *APV* for phrases to suggest an alternative point of view and *D* for phrases to disagree.

1 ✔ I'd like to … but I'd prefer … APV
2 ◯ I don't get why … ______
3 ◯ If you don't like … we can … ______
4 ◯ I think it's better to … ______
5 ◯ It isn't right … ______
6 ◯ I don't think … ______
7 ◯ Another thing to consider … ______
8 ◯ We can still … we just … ______

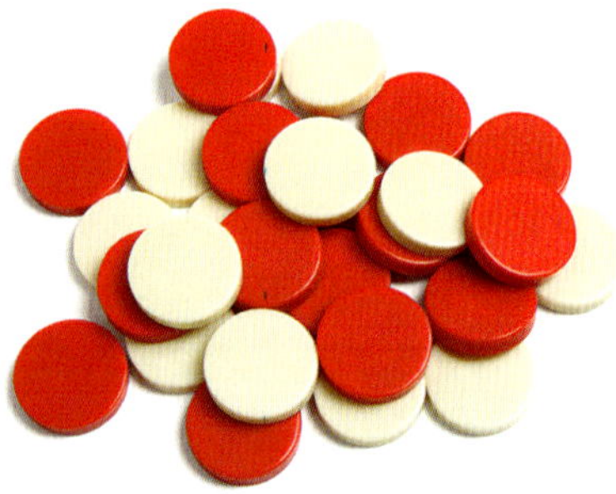

C Imagine you're going on vacation with a friend and you want to take some games. Think and make notes.

1 Which four games would you like to take?
2 Are they games to play by yourself or with other players?
3 Why do you think they're good games for a vacation?
4 Are there any games you definitely wouldn't take? If so, why?

D Discuss with your friend using phrases from **B**. Do you agree?

Reflect
Did I listen and respond to the points my friend made?

How well did you meet the challenge of Unit 6? Read and respond.

My Planning Sheet

We're all good at some things. I'm good at …	And we all need to improve some things. I need to work on …

We can always work to improve. Even when we are good at something, we can get better!

My plan to improve my English is …

If my plan works, then I'll …

I'll know my plan is working when …

Hello! Remember me? I'm Guan. I've spent a lot of time playing games as I like their graphics and design. What do you think I design? Find out in Unit 7!

UNIT 5

UNIT 6

Yesterday's

Find the differences

a

b

Vacation Fun

and then tell the stories.

a

b

UNIT 7

All About Ads

A Listen. Why is advertising important?

- [ ] **advertisement**
- [ ] **bargain**
- [ ] **billboard**
- [ ] **customer**
- 1 **discount**
- [ ] **persuade**
- [ ] **products**
- [ ] **profit**
- [ ] **quality**
- [ ] **value**

B Find and number the words in **A**. Then listen and check.

C Close your eyes. Listen, visualize, and say.

D Look and write. Then put the sentences in order of importance for you (1 = most important).

- [ ] All our p<u>roducts</u> are available online.
- [ ] Get a great d________ —40% off!
- [ ] It's an absolute b________ !
- [ ] Great v________ for money!
- [ ] High q________ service!
- [ ] Make a huge p________ !
- [ ] We take care of every single c________ !
- [ ] Like this a________ ? Come to our store!
- [ ] Can we p________ you to buy this?
- [ ] Large b________ available for advertising.

E Listen and write. Then watch and say.

Why Buy?

1 Bargains, ________
Come and spend.
2 ________
Buy for a friend!
3 ________
The ad—it's true!

4 ________
More for you!
5 ________
We want them, yes!
Come and buy.
We sell happiness!

F Pronunciation. Listen and say. Copy the intonation. Find three more sentences like these in the poem.

Come and spend! Buy for a friend!

🇺🇸	🇬🇧
donut advertisement	doughnut advert

Explore Language

A Listen and read. What products do the girls describe?

Guan: So you've watched different ads. What were they for?

Gabriela: Ours was for black toothpaste!

Ludka: And ours was a puzzle alarm clock.

Guan: Right! And what can you remember about these products?

Ludka: Well, the girl in the ad said you had to complete the puzzle to stop the alarm going off! She said she was getting up on time every day because the puzzle was challenging, and this made her feel wide awake.

Gabriela: Our ad told us to try this amazing new toothpaste. They said that it would remove stains from your teeth, even though the toothpaste is black!

Guan: Would you like to try these products out?

Ludka: We're not sure—what if you can't find the pieces to turn off the alarm clock! In my group, we thought that the puzzle should be easier, too.

Gabriela: I think it sounds fun! In our ad, people told the presenter that they'd never used a better toothpaste. Sami told us not to use it because it's so black! But I'd like to try it—the color wouldn't put *me* off. I'd have to warn my mom, though!

Grammar Reported Speech: Statements and Commands

B Look at **A**. Complete the table. How do the verbs change from direct speech to reported speech with *should?*

Reported Speech: Statements and Commands

Direct Speech	Reported Speech						
"It will remove stains from your teeth."	They	said	(that)	it	______ ______		stains from your teeth.
"The puzzle should be easier."	We	______	(that)	the puzzle	______ be		easier.
"We've never used a better toothpaste."	People	told	the presenter	______	they	______ never ______	a better toothpaste.

I saw it **yesterday.** → *He said he'd seen it* **the day before.**

Look

C Think and discuss. Then choose.

1 We use reported speech to report what someone said using their exact words / similar words.

2 We use *say* / *tell* + an infinitive verb to report commands.

D Listen and say.

E Read and write the reported speech statements.

1 "I've decided not to eat any more junk food."

She said that she had decided not to eat any more junk food.

2 "My favorite advertisements are the ones for sportswear."

He told us ______________________________.

3 "I'm interested in working in the advertising industry."

He said that ______________________________.

4 "We have to think more carefully about what we spend our money on."

She said that ______________________________.

5 "Stop putting billboards in the town," the mayor said.

The mayor told them ______________________________.

F Do you agree or disagree with the sentences in **E**? Do a class survey. Report your results.

"I'm interested in working in the advertising industry."

Margarita said that ...

What do advertisments sell, other than physical products?

A Listen to Naomi talk to her mom. What does she learn about advertising strategies?

2 ______________

3 ______________

4 ______________

1 promote

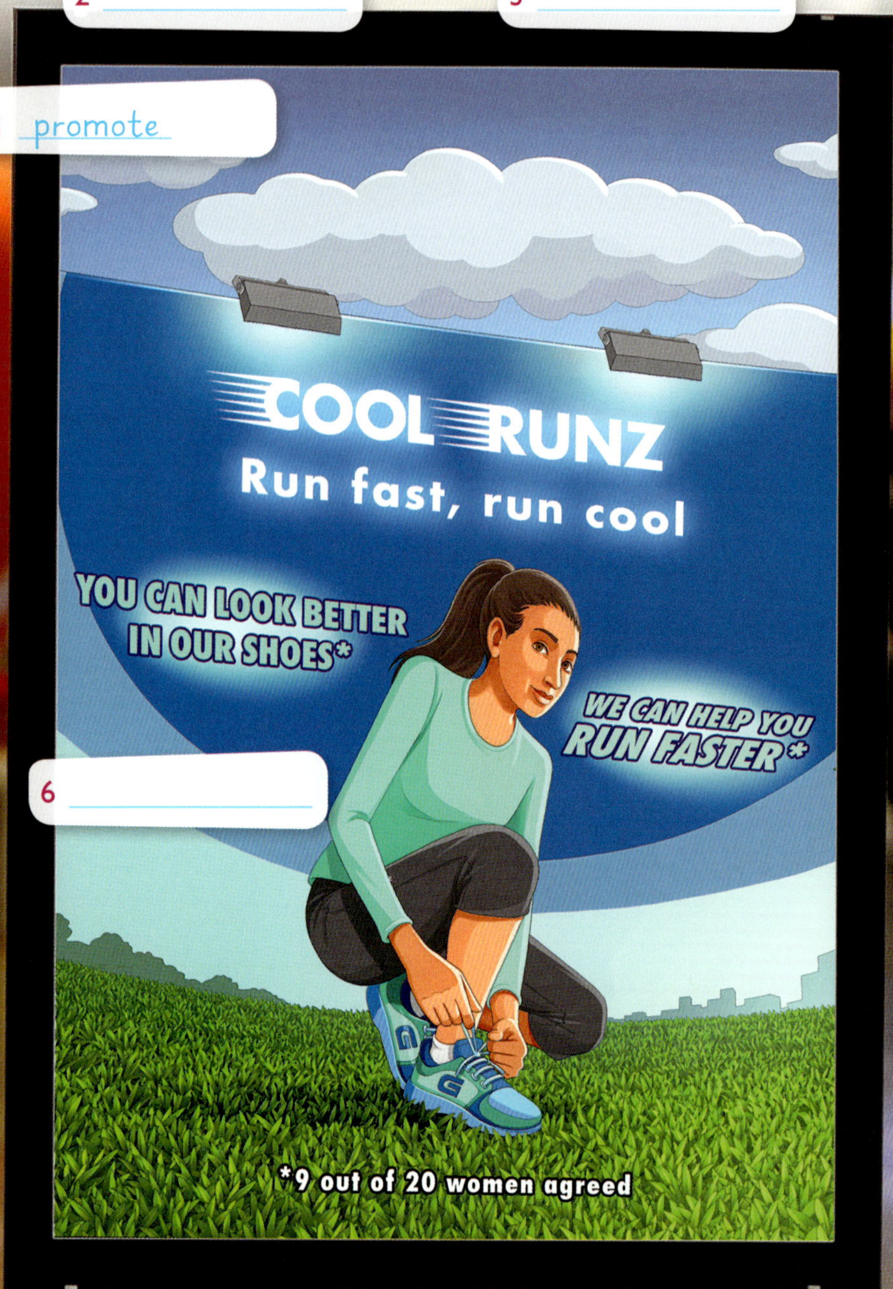

6 ______________

5 ______________

7 ______________

untrue or misleading information

8 ______________

B Look at the pictures and definition in **A** and write. Then listen and check.

brand **claims** **false impression** **image**
~~promote~~ **slogan** **small print** **target market**

C Read and complete the blog post.

Is It Real?

We see a lot of advertisements every day for all kinds of products made by big **1** brands but is what they're selling real? Think about it. You see an **2** ________ and it has to look perfect in order to **3** ________ the product. But many advertisements are giving us a **4** ________ because they aren't about real people or maybe the **5** ________ they make aren't true. They know what appeals to their **6** ________ so they use the pictures and a fun **7** ________ to make you think that their product is cool and to get you to spend your money. But, for the truth, remember to read the **8** ________ carefully!

D Now listen to Gail's podcast. What problems and solutions does she mention?

E Listen again. Write *True*, *False*, or *Doesn't Say*.

1 Everyone sees 5,000 ads every day. False
2 Companies promote products that we don't need. ________
3 Some packaging cannot be recycled. ________
4 Plastic is killing marine life. ________
5 Food which isn't sold can be given away so it isn't wasted. ________
6 All new products should be made from parts of old products. ________

What have you and your family bought over the last month that you don't need? What are the effects of people buying so many things?

Explore Language

A Listen and read. What's the TV quiz about?

Welcome to Ask the Experts! Today's show is about ads.

We asked:

- how many marketing messages a person received every day.
- what people thought the most annoying ads were.
- which product was top in the sports and outdoors category.
- where in the world 50% of the total advertising budget is on digital media.

We questioned:

- whether people remembered the advertising messages.

We wanted to know:

- if people knew how much money is spent on advertising in one year worldwide.

B Look at **A**. Complete the table. Which words come after the reporting verb in *Yes/No* questions?

Reported Speech: Questions

Direct Questions	Reported Questions						
"Which product was top in the sports category?"	We	asked	(them)	______	product	______	top in the sports category.
"Do you remember the advertising messages?"	We	questioned		______	people	______	the advertising messages.
"Do you know how much money is spent on advertising?"		wanted ______		if		knew	how much money is spent on advertising.

*I asked **her** if she liked the ad.*
= I asked if she liked the ad.

Look

C Think and discuss. Then choose.

1 We use reported / direct questions to say what someone asked without using quotation marks.

D Listen and say.

E Read the questions a student asked Guan. Write reported questions.

1 "When do you watch advertisements on TV?" (ask)

I asked him when he watched advertisements on TV.

2 "Do you prefer TV or billboard ads?" (want / to know)

I ______________________________.

3 "Why are there so many ads nowadays?" (wonder)

I ______________________________.

4 "Is the way products are promoted going to change in the future?" (question)

I ______________________________.

5 "How can people make sure the claims in ads are accurate?" (ask)

I ______________________________.

F Ask and answer three questions about a product you use. Then write about the questions your friend asked and your answers.

Why did you start using this product?

My friend told me about it.

She asked me why I started using this product.. I told her ...

Write About It

A Read the essay. How does the writer feel about advertising?

Is Advertising a Good Thing? Discuss.

Today, there are advertisements all around us. I think this is a great way of giving us choices and showing us what is out there.

People often complain that we have too many advertisements, but they are a useful way for companies to show us what is available to buy or to announce a new product. Most advertisements tell you about the different features of a product so you can get the information very quickly without having to search online or to read too much. We can see the latest ideas and newest inventions so we can understand what the products can offer. This helps us to make better decisions about the products we buy.

In addition, companies compete with each other and the advertisements let you see who offers the best quality, the lowest price, and so on. So you get a really wide choice and can buy the best thing for what you need.

Another point to consider is that advertisements are a modern form of art. Advertisements can be extremely creative. They can tell fabulous stories and can give powerful messages. They can make you laugh or cry. It is interesting, funny, and informative to see advertisements all around us and they make our lives brighter.

All in all, I believe advertisements are a very good thing and, in my view, life would be a little boring without them.

B Look at the structure of the essay. Read and answer.

1 What is the purpose of each paragraph? Write the paragraph numbers.

a. ☐ a conclusion
b. ☐ an introduction
c. ☐ reasons why advertisements are interesting
d. ☐ ☐ reasons why having a lot of advertisements is a good idea

2 Does the essay give facts, opinions, or both? Why? ______

3 Is the writing formal or informal? How do you know? ______

______

4 Does the last paragraph summarize ideas from the essay or introduce a new idea?

______

C Look at the language in the essay. Read and respond.

1 Make a list of the adjectives. great, ______

______

2 Are any of the adjectives the same? ______

3 Are any of the adjectives negative? ______

4 Which adjectives in the essay are synonyms? ______

5 Choose three adjectives in the essay and think of others with similar meanings.

______

D Think and discuss. Brainstorm some disadvantages of advertising using one of the Generating Ideas techniques.

E Plan your essay called *Switch Off Advertising*. Use your ideas in **D** and one of the Planning techniques.

Paragraph	Purpose	Ideas
1.	Introduction	
2.	Reasons 1 and 2	
3.	Reasons 3 and 4	
4.	Summary	

F Write a first draft of your essay. Then think about how you've organized the information and revise it.

G Now write your essay.

Read and Respond
Ask your friend to read your essay. Do your arguments persuade them?

Talk About It

A Watch and listen. Do you think Maria is right for the job?

Watch
Who do Linda and Maria look at during the conversation? Why

B Watch again. Match the phrases. Then write *QS* (qualities and skills) or *E* (experience).

1 I always give	a. my main strengths …	
2 I'm a very committed	b. with …	
3 I always	c. of hard work …	
4 I'm not afraid	d. person …	
5 One of my skills is	e. stick with …	
6 Being organized is one of	f. 100% …	QS
7 My experience …	g. in …	
8 I collaborated	h. being able to listen …	

C Imagine you're going to be interviewed to be a student community leader. What skills, qualities, and experience do you have? Think and plan.

Qualities	Skills	Experience

D Take turns to interview each other. Use phrases from **B**.

Can you tell me what your main strengths are?

Being hard-working is one of my main strengths.

Reflect
Did I use positive, persuasive language?

How well did you meet the challenge of Unit 7? Read and respond.

MONTHLY GOAL REFLECTION

My goal from Unit 6 was to …

Overall, I rate my effort towards my goal as …

To achieve my goal, I …

Other things I learned or improved this month …

Next month

I will continue to work on this goal. I will set myself a new goal.

My plan now is to …

Hello! Remember me? I'm Ludka and I'd like to work in advertising because I like design and images. What beautiful designs are there in nature? Find out in Unit 8!

UNIT 8

What Are the Odds?

A Listen. Which three photos does the group talk about?

- [ ] **angle**
- [ ] **divide**
- [ ] **even number**
- 1 **hexagon**
- [ ] **multiply**
- [ ] **odd number**
- [ ] **prime number**
- [ ] **sequence**
- [ ] **spirals**
- [ ] **symmetry**

B Find and number the words in **A**. Then listen and check.

C Close your eyes. Listen, visualize, and say.

D Look and write.

1 The space where two straight lines join or cross each other is an angle

2 Each of these numbers is an ______ : 21, 23, 25, 27, 29

3 ______ is when two halves are exactly the same

4 Each of these is an ______ : 10, 12, 14, 16, 18

5 The Fibonacci ______ is nature's growth pattern

6 × means ______ in: 10 × 2 = 20

7 Each of these is a ______ : 2, 3, 5, 7, 11, 13

8 ÷ means ______ in: 10 ÷ 2 = 5

9 A six-sided shape is a ______

10 Shapes that go round and round: ______

E Listen and choose. Then watch and say.

I Love Numbers

I have numbers on my mind
1 Symmetry / Sequence 's in patterns
I find.

In my sequence, 2 multiply / divide
Odd and 3 prime / even, then apply!

Numbers, numbers!

My number's 4 odd / prime.
What's the rule?
Divide just by itself and one. That's cool!

Two lines joined. What did you get?
5 An angle / A spiral at the point
they met.

Math in nature? Bring it on!
A honeycomb is a 6 sequence / hexagon.

Sunflowers, insects, a galaxy?
7 Spirals / Symmetry in nature, come
and see.

F Pronunciation. Listen and say. Copy the consonant clusters. Find other words with consonant clusters in the poem.

symmetry **multiply** **prime**

Explore Language

A Listen and read. What information does Adam give Ludka about eclipses?

Adam: Did you know that the sun is about 400 times bigger than the moon, and it's also about 400 times further away?

Ludka: Really?

Adam: Yeah, that's why they look the same size when they're seen from Earth.

Ludka: Right! And the angle of light from the sun affects how much light and shade we get, doesn't it?

Adam: Yes. But during a solar eclipse, the moon passes in front of the sun so it goes dark, see? The sun has often been covered completely—it's called a total eclipse.

Ludka: Doesn't what you see depend on where you're positioned on Earth?

Adam: Yes, in most places it's only a partial eclipse. They're amazing to see. But you can't look directly at the eclipse as you can be blinded by it.

Ludka: Oh, that's bad! How did you get this photo then?

Adam: Oh, that's not mine. It was taken by a professional, with an expensive camera.

B Look at **A**. Complete the table. Which verb is in all passive sentences?

Passives: Present and Past

It	________			called		a total eclipse.
	was			________	by	a professional.
You	can	________		________		it.
The sun	________	often	________	covered		completely.

The moon covers the sun.
The sun is covered by the moon.

Remember

C Think and discuss. Then choose.

1 We use the passive when we're more interested in the action than in who or what did the action. True / False

2 We often use the passive when reporting something or making an impersonal statement. True / False

D Listen and say.

E Complete the sentences using the correct form of the passive.

1 People have studied the symmetry of the solar system for centuries.

The symmetry of the solar system has been studied for centuries.

2 Scientists measured the distance between the sun and the planets accurately.

The distance between the sun and the planets ______________________.

3 You can see five planets from Earth without a telescope.

Five planets ______________________.

4 Astronauts use the spaceship to practice before the launch.

The spaceship ______________________.

5 They might build a new observatory in Australia.

______________________.

F Think and discuss. What do you know about space?

In 2017, a new solar system was discovered.

The first space shuttle was launched in 1981.

How does math link to different aspects of our lives?

A Listen to Jung-mi and Hiroki talk about a research project. What information surprises them?

1 data

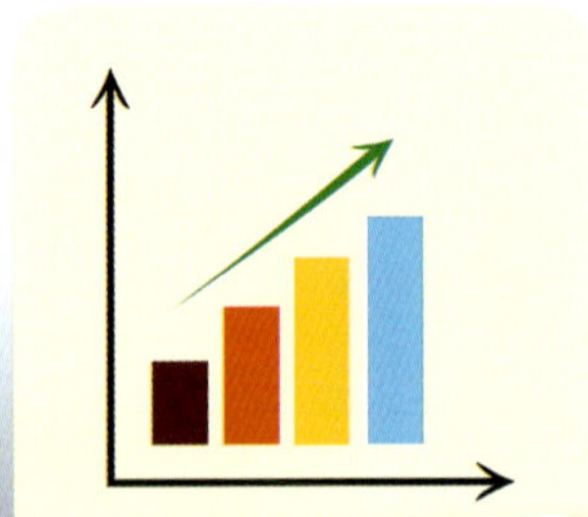
2 ______

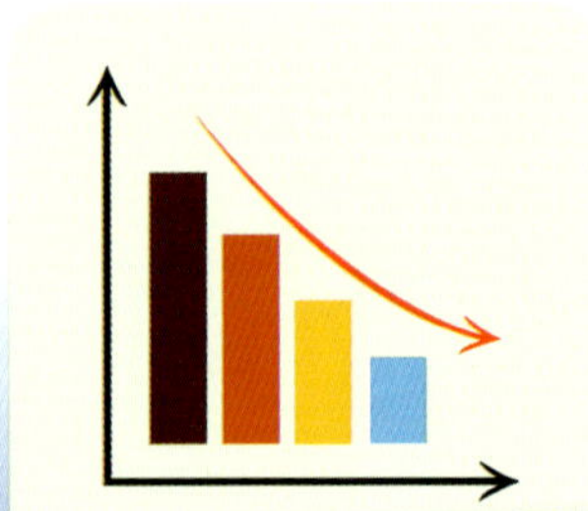
3 ______

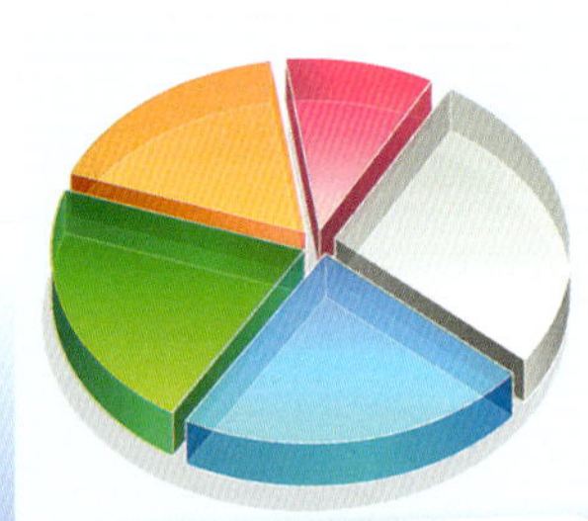
4 ______

5 ______

6 ______

7 ______

8 ______

9 ______

a gradual change or development that produces a particular result

10 ______

B Look at the pictures and definition in **A** and write. Then listen and check.

average chart ~~data~~ fall percentage
reach a peak rise statistics stay stable trend

C Read and complete using the information in the chart.

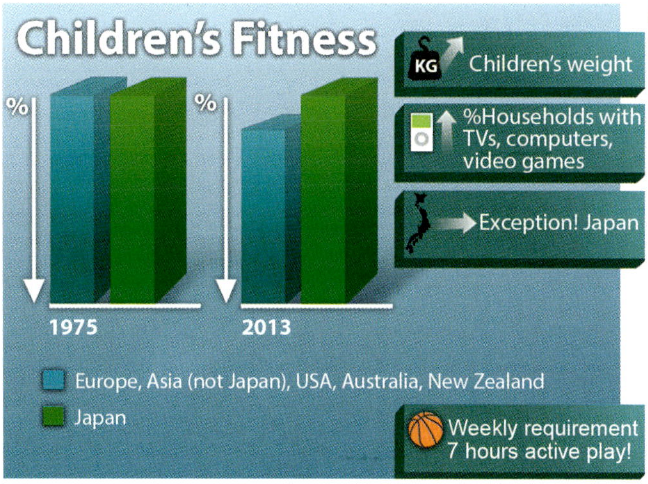

1 This chart shows that in many countries, there has been a f________ of 15% in children's fitness since 1975.

2 The only country that is different in the areas analyzed is Japan, which has s________ .

3 The s________ also show that there has been a r________ in children's weight over the same period.

4 The problem has not yet r________ so the situation will get worse.

5 The data suggests that there is a higher p________ of homes which have TVs and computers.

6 All children should be getting an a________ of 60 minutes active play a day.

D Now listen to a radio program. Why does Ms. Pérez say that math is everywhere?

E Listen again. Answer the questions.

1 What example does Ms. Pérez give of using math every day?

When she goes shopping and buys things.

2 How can data help stores stock their shelves?

____

3 Does Ms. Pérez think it's normal for stores to run out of bananas? Why or why not?

____

4 Why does it matter how many babies are born in a country?

____

5 What example does Ms. Pérez give when talking about a country's population? ________

6 Why do people need to think about new schools when they build new houses?

____

How is math useful in your life?
How can math be used to help solve problems in your community?

A Listen and read. Why is data important?

Vincent: Adam—you're using your phone AGAIN.

Adam: What? I'm just looking up train times …

Vincent: You know, I read recently that every time you search a website online, data is being collected—data about you! Companies use the information to send you targeted advertisements about things you like—your favorite jeans or video games. Some companies collect data on the TV shows people watch. The data will be analyzed to help them decide whether to make another series or not, or which characters to change. They're saying that data analysis is going to be used more and more.

Adam: That sounds good, doesn't it? In the future, TV shows I like won't be canceled if they've analyzed my data!

Vincent: But it's like everything we do is being watched.

Adam: True. I guess I do use my phone for everything. Hmm, so, now we know we're being watched, how will the data be collected? And what do you think the results will be?

Vincent: Good questions …

Adam: Well, after this, I'm going to be sent a ton of ads about trains from this station!

analyzed	analysed

B Look at **A**. Complete the table. Which verb form do we use for the main verb?

Passives: Future Forms

Data analysis	is going to	be	________	more and more.
The data	________		________	to help them decide.
How	________	the data	________	collected?

Look

Someone will send you ads to your phone.
Ads will be sent to your phone.

C Think and discuss. Then choose.

1 We often use the passive in reports or factual information where we want to be objective / personal.

2 We can / can't use some verbs in the passive, for example *live, die, stay*.

D Listen and say.

E Read the report. Write the sentences or questions with a future form passive.

1 More white sneakers / buy / girls than boys / next year

More white sneakers will be bought by girls than by boys next year.

2 Which / video games / play / most

____

3 Jeans / not / going to / wear / as much

____

4 Homework / correct / robots not teachers

____

5 Big computers / not / buy / in the same numbers as today

____

6 More apps / going to / design / teenagers

____

F Think about current trends. Make predictions about the future. Talk with a friend.

I think video games will be played less in the future because ...

Children won't be taken to school by bus ...

A Read the biography. What's unusual about the mathematician?

The Games Master: John Horton Conway

John Horton Conway is a modern mathematician who is important because he invented an extraordinary computer game. He has been described as a mixture of a mathematician, a musician, and an artist.

He was born in Liverpool in the UK in 1937. He was interested in numbers from the age of two. At school he was excellent at math and went to Cambridge University. Then he went to work at Princeton University in the USA.

In 1970, he created the *Game of Life*, a zero-player game that used artificial intelligence instead of human players. It helped create a new type of math and is used in computer programs and coding today.

He has written lots of books and received several prizes for his work. I think he is interesting because he studies the science of games. I would love to make a career from playing games!

Princeton University

B Look at the structure of the biography. Read and write why each feature is important.

1 Why the writer thinks the person is of interest To give the reader a purpose for reading.

2 Background: date and place of birth, childhood, education ______

3 Time phrases, dates, connecting phrases ______

4 A photograph and a caption ______

5 Important moments, events, and achievements ______

6 The writer's opinion of the person ______

C Look at the language of the biography. Complete the table with examples from the biography.

Facts	Supporting example
Why Conway is important	1 He invented an extraordinary computer game.
Why the *Game of Life* is important	2 3
What Conway has achieved in his life	4
Why you think Conway is important	5

D Think and discuss. Choose a subject for a biography. What do you need to know about this person? Use one of the Generating Ideas techniques.

E Plan your biography. Use your notes in **D** and one of the Planning techniques.

F Write a first draft, then revise it. Use a checklist.

G Now write your revised biography.

Read and Respond

Ask your friend to read your biography. Is the information ordered logically?

A Watch and listen. Which number surprises Wade?

Watch
How does Wade use graphics to make his presentation interesting?

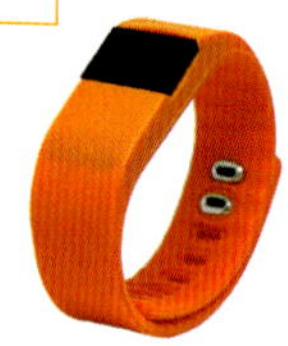

B Watch again. What effect do the phrases have in the presentation? Check (✔).

	Engage the audience	Motivate and incentivize	Encourage reflection	Create interest in a fact
1 Imagine a world with no …	✔			
2 Impossible, isn't it?				
3 Did you know that that …?				
4 It's good to help people, isn't it?				
5 Take a minute to think about …				
6 This surprises me.				
7 Do you know how … you are?				
8 Let's …				

C Think about the numbers in your day. Use these ideas and your own. Think and plan.

dates/times | daily routine | family | food/meals
activities | school subjects | in town | things you saw/said

Interesting facts
Things the audience can think about
Something personal/surprising

Reflect
Did I encourage my audience to reflect?

D Practice with your friends. Then share with the class. Take notes and give feedback.

How well did you meet the challenge of Unit 8? Read and respond.

3 · 2 · 1

3 new facts I learned in this unit

1

2

3

2 "Ah-ha!" moments I had

1

2

1 big question I still have

1

Hello! Remember me? I'm Vincent. I really like using math to solve problems. Now I have to make a big decision! What will help me decide? Find out in Unit 9!

UNIT 7 UNIT 8

Word Scramble Race

Team A

1

2

3

4

Team B

1

2

3

4

HOW TO PLAY

1 Play in groups of four. Divide each group into two pairs. Your teacher will give each pair an envelope with word cards.
2 In pairs, make four sentences from the words.
3 One of the sentences is false. Discuss with your friend which one it is.
4 Look at the sentences from the other pair and decide which sentence is false. The pair to find the false sentence the fastest wins.
5 Discuss all the sentences as a group.

UNIT 9

Make Up Your Mind

A Listen. What decision does Annette want to talk about?

- ☐ brainstorm the options
- ☐ consider the consequences
- ☐ decide on a solution
- ☐ define the problem
- 1 evaluate your ideas
- ☐ learn from your mistakes
- ☐ make a decision
- ☐ regret

3 think about what will happen as a result of something you do

5 choose a way to solve a problem

B Find and number the words in **A**. Then listen and check.

C Close your eyes. Listen, visualize, and say.

middle school/ high school	secondary school

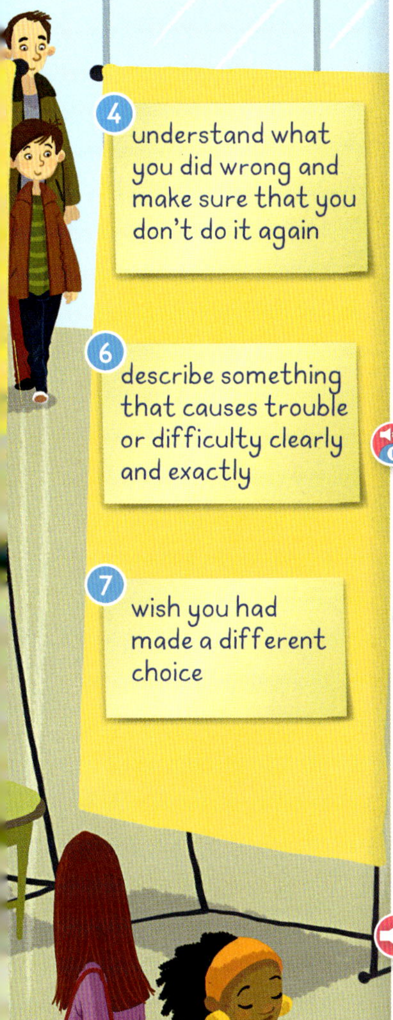

D Look, choose, and write. Then read and write the letters.

1 define the problem [e] → 2 ______ [ ] → 3 ______ [ ] → 4 ______ [ ] → 5 ______ [ ]

a. Attend Fitness Club / go running every morning / go swimming

b. I'll regret it if I don't try my best to get fit.

c. Decided to go running with a friend (learned from mistakes—don't like running on own)

d. Fitness Club fun but expensive / running is free but need a friend / swimming fun but pool not near

e. Need to get fit to be selected for basketball team

E Listen and write. Then watch and say.

Make Up My Mind

Define the 1 problem —yes or no?
Define it logically—where shall I go?

Brainstorm the 2 ______ —one, two, three.
Brainstorm—A, B, C, and D.

Evaluate your 3 ______ —bad or good?
Evaluate—do I think I should?

Consider the 4 ______ —nothing to regret?
Consider them carefully—I can't decide yet!

Decide on a 5 ______ —it's now or never!
Decide so I can say—it's my best decision ever!

F Pronunciation. Listen and say. Copy the linking. Think of other examples of linking like these.

the (y) options | evaluate your ideas | I can'(t) decide | decide on

Explore Language

A Listen and read. What did Annette learn? Did she enjoy her day?

1

Annette: Phew! That was a long wait, Yousef.

Yousef: If you'd come earlier, Annette, we wouldn't have waited in line so long.

Annette: I know! I'm sorry. I hope we like it after all that!

2

Annette: Lunch was so expensive!

Yousef: If you'd brought your own lunch, it would have been cheaper.

Annette: I know. Your lunch looks really nice!

3

Annette: Well, I've learned from my mistakes today. Don't be late and pack my own lunch!

Yousef: But you still had a good time, didn't you?

Annette: Sure. If I hadn't come, I would have regretted it. I would have missed all this, um … fun!

B Look at **A**. Complete the table. What verb form comes after *if*?

Third Conditional: Statements

If	you	had/ ______	come	earlier,	we	wouldn't ______	______	waited	in line so long.
			______	your own lunch,	it			been	cheaper.
	I	______	come,		I			______	it.

I would have been OK.
I would've been OK.
I'd've been OK.

Look

C Think and discuss. Then choose.

1 We use the third conditional to describe a situation that happened / didn't happen in the past.

2 When we use the third conditional, we're describing the actual result / imagined result of a situation.

3 We often use the third conditional to express regret or complain about something. True / False

D Listen and say.

E Read the regrets and considerations. Complete with the correct form of the verbs.

1 If I hadn't worked (not work) hard, I 'd have failed (fail) my exam.

2 If I ______ (not get up) late, I ______ (not miss) the bus today.

3 I ______ (send) my cousin a card if I ______ (remember) her birthday.

4 I ______ (learn) to speak a different language if I ______ (live) in a different country.

5 If I ______ (know) about the art competition, I ______ (paint) a picture.

6 If I ______ (not join) the club, I ______ (not meet) my best friend!

7 I ______ (call) my mom if I ______ (remember) to take my cell phone.

8 If I ______ (go) for a run, I ______ (feel) much better.

F Write new sentences for the *if* clauses in **E**. Then compare with a friend. Whose sentences are the most interesting?

If I hadn't worked hard,
my teacher would have been upset.

If I hadn't gotten up late,
I'd have had breakfast.

How do the decisions we make affect other people?

A Listen to Fatima talk to Lily about decision-making in her family. What kinds of decisions do Fatima's family make?

1 fit in with

2 ______

3 ______

4 ______

5 ______

6 ______

get the chance to say what you think about something

7 ______

the influence that other people of your own age have on you

8 ______

9 ______

B Look at the pictures and definitions in **A** and write. Then listen and check.

be fair | control your emotions | ~~fit in with~~ | get your own way | have your say | independence | individual identity | peer pressure | pros and cons

C Read the school poster and complete.

BE BRAVE

YES! YOU CAN

1 Try to develop your _independence_ and do things for yourself.

2 Be __________ and listen to everyone's opinion even if it takes longer.

3 Take time to look at the __________ and __________ before making a decision.

4 Don't give in to peer __________ —develop your own ideas and individual __________ .

5 Keep calm and control your __________ even if you don't get your own __________ .

6 Have your __________ but then try to __________ in with the group decision.

DREAM BIG

YOU ARE AWESOME

D Now listen to Professor Jackson. How does the brain affect how 11- to 13-year-olds feel and act?

E Listen again. Write *True* or *False*.

1 After 13, the brain doesn't change any more. __________

2 According to the radio program, children aged between 11 and 13 feel more self-confident than before. _False_

3 Understanding different points of view can make decision-making difficult. __________

4 They make decisions on a logical basis more than on an emotional basis. __________

5 Pre-teens don't have strategies to deal with tricky situations. __________

6 Brain changes at this age help children become smarter. __________

How do you make decisions in your family?
How can children be involved in decisions about their community?

Explore Language

A Listen and read. What new experience did Grace have last week?

1

2

Grace: Last week, I decided to say "yes" to everything that people asked me to do.

Ana: That's exciting! But if someone had told you to do something dangerous, would you have done it?

Grace: Of course not! Nobody asked me to do dangerous stuff and I wouldn't have taken any silly risks. I just did it for fun.

Tony: And was it?!

Grace: Well, there were pros and cons. Sometimes I felt nervous, but it made me do things that normally I wouldn't have done. Like going zip-lining.

Ana: But what would you have done if you'd fallen?

Grace: Oh, I wore the right equipment so I was safe. It's a bit scary, though.

Tony: You're brave …

Grace: Honestly, it's fun. If I'd asked you to come with me, what would you have said?

Ana: I'm afraid I'd have said "No!"

Tony: Me too! I like adventures but not heights!

Grace: But …

Ana: No way. I like to keep my feet on the ground!

B Look at **A**. Complete the table. Is the position of the *if* clause always the same?

Third Conditional: Questions

What		______	you	have done	______	you	'd	______ ?
If	someone	had	______	you to do something dangerous,	______	you	______ done	it?
	I	______	asked	you to come with me,	what	______	you	have ______ ?

Don't use *would* in the *if* clause.

Watch Out

C Think and discuss. Then choose.

1 We use third conditional questions to ask about situations that happened in the past. True / False

2 We use third conditional questions to ask about the possible consequences of an imagined situation. True / False

D Listen and say.

E Read the situations and complete the questions. Sometimes there is more than one answer. Then ask and answer.

1 I regret going to the beach on vacation.
Where would you have gone _if you hadn't gone to the beach_ ?

2 I didn't know you were waiting for me.
Would you have come sooner ______________________ ?

3 I ate really unhealthily and I felt terrible.
If you'd eaten more healthily, ______________________ ?

4 I hurt my leg, so I couldn't do any of the activities.
What activities would you have done ______________________ ?

5 I lost my wallet, so I didn't buy anything.
If you hadn't lost your wallet, ______________________ ?

F Think about three decisions you made this year. What would have happened if you had made a different decision? Talk to a friend.

I decided to learn French.

If you hadn't decided to learn French, would ...?

Write About It

A Read the article. Check (✓) the points the article mentions.

1 ◯ Writing lists

2 ◯ Weekly schedule

3 ◯ Setting an alarm clock

4 ◯ Talking to your parents

Keep Your Eye on the Clock: Time Management for Kids

How many times have you been late for something? How many times have you run out of time and not been able to finish your homework? How often do you say: "I would have done it if I'd had more time!"? Managing your own time is a vital skill which will help you be successful, not only at school, but throughout your whole life. Here are some tips to help you.

1 Make a schedule of your week and stick it on the wall. Write in all the things you have to do, like school, clubs, weekend activities, and helping with household chores. Make it a work of art!

2 Write or print out a list of all your homework assignments for the week. Make sure you know when the deadlines are. Check off each one when you've done it.

3 Decide with your parents how much screen time you can have. Write this on your schedule, too.

So, no more excuses. Keep your eye on the clock and get organized! Your life will be more efficient: you'll have the time to do what you need to do and what you want to do. It's easy—you won't regret it!

schedule | timetable

B Look at the structure of the article. Read and complete.

Feature	Example	How it makes the article clear
1 An interesting title		
2 A list of numbered points	1, 2, 3	
3 Short statements		
4 A statement of the end result		

C Look at the language of the article. Match the features to the examples.

1 Short statements

2 Imperatives

3 Personal questions

a. Keep your eye on the clock and get organized!

b. How often do you say: "I'd have done it if I'd had more time!"?

c. So, no more excuses.

Different genres of writing use different techniques, such as short sentences and bullet points, to engage the reader.

Process Writing
Editing and Publishing, p143

D Think and discuss. You're going to write an article called *How Can You Make Good Decisions in Your Life?* Use one of the Generating Ideas techniques.

E Plan your article. Use your ideas in **D** and one of the Planning techniques.

Title	Introductory paragraph	Instructions list / Tips / Points	Conclusion / Summary

F Write a first draft. Then review it using a checklist.

How Can You Make Good Decisions in Your Life?

Read and Respond
Ask your friend to read your article. Ask him/her to follow the instructions. What's the result?

G Now write your article. Re-read and edit it. Then publish it.

A Watch and listen. What does Wade think is an important decision?

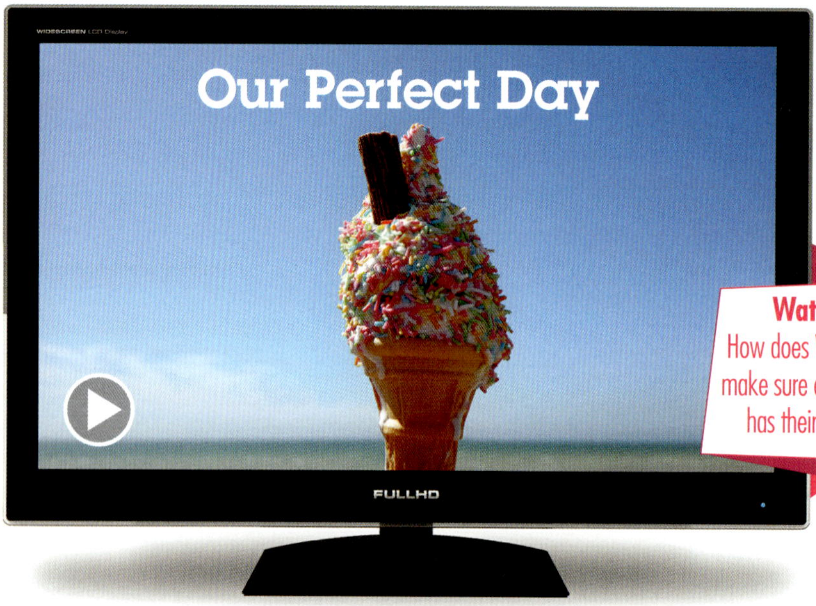

Watch
How does Veronica make sure everyone has their say?

B Watch again. Put the phrases in the order you hear them.

a. ☐ Do you agree?
b. ☐ What do you think?
c. ☐ What do you think of Maria's idea?
d. ☐ Do you think that's a good idea?
e. 1 What would you like to do …?
f. ☐ Perhaps we should …

C Imagine you're going to spend a day with two friends. What do you want to do and why? Think and plan.

Morning	Afternoon	Evening

D Talk with your friends using phrases from B. Plan your perfect day together.

I'd like to go on a roller coaster. What do you think?

Perhaps we should go to the movies and see a 3D movie.

Reflect
Was everyone included in the conversation?

How well did you meet the challenge of Unit 9? Read and respond.

My Favorite Mistakes

Means
I
Start
To
Acquire
Knowledge
Experience
Skills

Two mistakes I made in this unit that moved my learning on are …

Two things (knowledge) I learned about decision-making are …

Two things (experience and skills) I learned to say or do in English are …

Two things I want to work on next month are …

This is your goal.

Hello! Remember us? We're Ana and Tony Moreno. Our company organizes trips for students to visit schools in other countries. Which country are we going to next? Find us in Unit 10!

UNIT 10

Take the Lead

A Listen. What's the students' end-of-year-project about?

- [ ] can-do attitude
- 1 encourage
- [ ] gut feeling
- [ ] inspire
- [ ] mentor
- [ ] positive influence
- [ ] respect
- [ ] role model

B Find and number the words in A. Then listen and check.

C Close your eyes. Listen, visualize, and say.

D Look and write. Then complete the column for you.

Important people in my life	Who?
1 My role model is someone I want to be like.	a.
2 My m__________ is my experienced and trusted advisor.	b.
3 I r__________ him/her for his/her qualities and abilities.	c.
4 This person always e__________ me to do my best.	d.
5 This person i__________ me to study harder.	e.
6 This person has always had a p__________ influence on me.	f.
7 This person has a c__________ attitude, always thinking they'll succeed.	g.
8 This person knows instinctively what is right—they follow their g__________ feeling.	h.

E Listen and write. Then watch and say.

Let's Look to the Future

I believe in myself.
I believe in you.
Let's look to the future.
Wow! What a view!

You're my 1 role model.
You're so clever.
You 2 __________ me.
You're the best friend ever!

You're my 3 __________ .
I 4 __________ you, too.
You do your best
And 5 __________ me, too!

F Pronunciation. Listen and say. Copy the sentence stress. How does it change the meaning?

You're the best friend ever.

You're the best friend ever.

You're the best friend ever.

Explore Language

A Listen and read. What kind of people is Sofia talking about?

🇺🇸	🇬🇧
regular people	ordinary people

Mr. Moreno: So, who do you think are great leaders, Sofia?

Sofia: Well, in the past, there were some great leaders in Egypt like Hatshepsut, the second female pharaoh. And scientists can also be leaders, like Dr. Ali Moustafa Mosharafa. He even corresponded with Albert Einstein!

Mr. Moreno: What about now? And who will we be following in the future?

Sofia: Hmm, people like Roger Federer and Beyoncé. Some celebrities have millions of followers on social media …

Mr. Moreno: Do you think celebrities are good role models?

Sofia: Some can be. But some people are just famous for being famous—they haven't really done anything inspiring.

Mr. Moreno: You're right. I hope people won't only be following celebrities in the future. I hope they'll be learning more about regular hard-working people who do amazing things.

Sofia: Well, I'll be feeling inspired by the end of this trip, I'm sure! This time next week I'll be looking to discover what amazing things I can achieve.

Mr. Moreno: Good for you!

B Look at **A**. Complete the table. What verb form comes after *will be*?

Future Progressive

Who	______	we	be	______	in the future?
I	'll			______	inspired by the end of this trip!
People	______	only	______	following	celebrities in the future.

Adverbs go between *will* and *be*.

Look

C Think and discuss. Then choose.

1 We use the future progressive to talk about a finished action / an action in progress at a point in the future.

2 We use the future progressive with *this time* + a future time phrase to say the period of time when something will be in progress / finished.

D Listen and say.

E Read and complete.

1 In the future, she'll be working (working) with inspiring leaders.

2 This time next week, I ______________ (swim) in a competition.

3 When I'm older, I ______________ (not live) in the same house.

4 This time next year, I ______________ (not study) at the same school.

5 What ______________ you ______________ (do) at 7:00 p.m.?

6 By the time you're 25, do you think you ______________ (live) in a different place?

7 ______________ you still ______________ (sing) when you're at college?

8 I hope we ______________ (make) mistakes when we're studying in the USA.

F Read the prompts and make sentences for yourself. Then talk to your friend.

In the future … | This time next week … | On Tuesday … | When I'm older … | Next month …

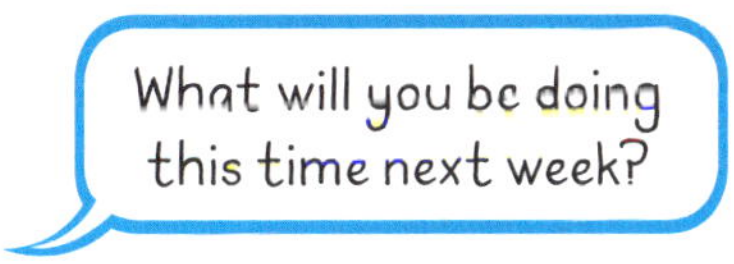

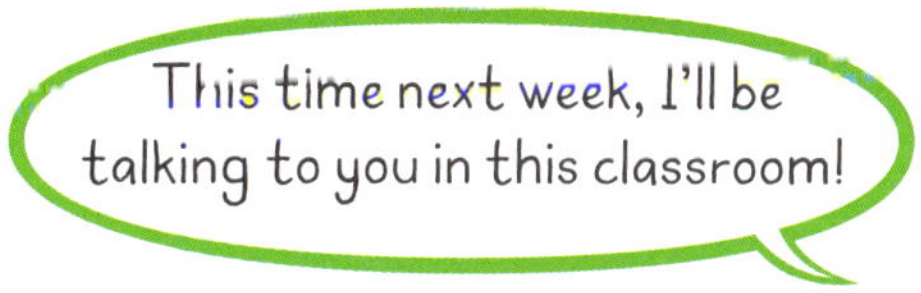

Can anyone be a leader?

A Listen to André talk to his mentor, Patrick. Does André believe he can be a good leader? Why?

1 set a good example

showing or expressing strong beliefs, interest or enthusiasm

2 ______

3 ______

4 ______

5 ______

6 ______

enthusiasm and determination to work hard at something

7 ______

a person who does not tell lies or cheat people or break the law

8 ______

B Look at the pictures and definitions in **A** and write. Then listen and check.

commitment   focus   honest   motivate
organizational skills   passionate   ~~set a good example~~   support

C Read and complete the advice.

How to Be a Good Leader

- Make sure you're 1 passionate so you can share your enthusiasm with others.
- Remember to 2 ______________ because people will be copying you.
- If you want to 3 ______ people, you need to give them 4 ______ in what they want to do.
- 5 ______ on achieving your goals—it's important to keep your promises and show 6 ______ if you want others to follow you.
- Be 7 ______ so that others always know what is real.
- Have good 8 ______________ so you can use your time and others' talents well.

D Now listen to Dev talk about Will Lourcey. What did Will do to help in his community?

E Listen again. Put the events in order.

a. [ ] Will and his friends collected cans of food.
b. [ ] Will contacted his friends and asked for their ideas.
c. [ ] Will thought of organizing monthly meals for hungry children.
d. [1] Will saw a man in the street asking for food.
e. [ ] Will and his friends started a child-run organization.
f. [ ] Will persuaded restaurants to give him food.

How can you become a good leader? Who would you lead? Why is good leadership important?

Explore Language

A Listen and read. What does Lucas want to do?

Mr. Hussein:	Tell me your ideas for next year's student exchange program, Lucas.
Lucas:	Well, I think the students from both schools will really benefit from it. We can schedule two weeks in the spring semester for students from your school to visit us next year. The students will attend classes at our school and they'll experience how we spend our free time. I'm going to find out how many students are interested. I think there'll be a lot. I'm having a meeting with the group later today.
Mr. Hussein:	It sounds great, but how much will this cost?
Lucas:	I'm not sure yet, but I'll be asking students to organize a fundraising event, which will support the program and help pay for the travel costs. I'd like Aaliyah to help me with this, if you agree?
Mr. Hussein:	Yes, agreed. She has excellent organizational skills and will support you.
Lucas:	Good. We'll also need to figure out where the students can stay.
Mr. Hussein:	There's a lot to think about. But I'm sure you will make it work.
Lucas:	Thank you. I'm determined to make sure other children have an exchange experience like this one. I hope it'll be a great success.
Mr Hussein:	Great. Now, let's say goodbye to this year's exchange students. We have cake!

B Look at **A**. Complete the table. Which verb form doesn't use an infinitive?

Review: Future Forms

I	________	________	find out	how many students are interested.
		having		a meeting with the group later today.
How much	________	this		________ ?
I hope	it	________	________	a great success.

Look

We can say *I'm going on vacation.* or *I'm going to go on vacation.*

C Think and discuss. Then match.

1 Hopes and thoughts
2 Future plans and intentions
3 Predictions (without evidence)
4 Predictions (with evidence)

a. *going to* + infinitive
b. present progressive
c. *will* + infinitive
d. *hope/think* + *will* + infinitive

D Listen and say.

E Read the email. Underline the time phrases. Then complete with the correct future form.

Hi, Felipe!

Only four days to go before our school event! We really hope we 1 'll make (make) more money for our school than last year. Tomorrow, we 2 ________ (finish) the design for the advertisement for our blog; we've already booked the IT room. I think we 3 ________ (ask) the teachers if they can help us. Mom 4 ________ (go) to the grocery store for us to get the food—we're 5 ________ (cook) the food on Friday after school. On Sunday, after it's all over, we 6 ________ (be) exhausted, but happy! I can't wait to visit the charity to give them our donation! I'll let you know how it goes.

Bye for now, Max

F Think about your life in the next six months and make notes. Then talk with a friend.

I'm going shopping on Saturday with my mom.

I hope we'll go to the beach this summer.

Write About It

A Read the blog post and comments. What does the writer of the blog post want to achieve? Does everyone agree to help?

Student Council Calling!

Hey, fellow students! We're in our final year now so we have to take the lead on things like helping with the school play or with training the sports teams. Well, if we can all work together with other schools, we can learn a lot and support each other. Are you in?

How about we set up an online group with our sister schools? We can exchange ideas and plans for how to organize the clubs and things we're interested in. Like how to mentor the younger kids or how to persuade the teachers when we want to do something new. Here are some suggestions:

- Exchange ideas on how to organize clubs
- Get new ideas, e.g. how to raise money for the school …
- Organize ways to support younger students

If you're a leader, let me know what you think. Great idea? Send comments!

Hey—fantastic idea count me in. 🙂 Don't have time to help—sorry. ☹ THX 4 this—when do we start?

B Look at the structure of the blog post. Match the features to the reasons.

1 have a title
2 use bullets, lists, graphs, images, no "wall of text"
3 include questions
4 include main idea in first paragraph
5 write in chatty style

a. to make sure you get comments
b. so that the reader wants to keep reading
c. to catch the reader's eye
d. for variety so the blog post is easy to read
e. to address the reader personally

C Look at the language in the blog post. Read and respond.

1 Write these sentences in a chatty style.

a. Dear classmates ______
b. So, if we are all willing to help, … ______
c. I suggest that we set up a new club. ______

2 Cross out the words you don't need.

a. Do you think this is a good idea?
b. Please do send your comments.
c. We don't have enough time. I am sorry.

D Think and discuss. You're going to write a blog post about a project or event. Choose a project or event that you'd like to organize and lead. Brainstorm lots of ideas using one of the Generating Ideas techniques.

E Plan your blog post. Use some of your ideas in D and one of the Planning techniques.

F Now write a first draft of your blog post. Then review it using a checklist.

G Write your blog post. Then check it using the Editing and Publishing questions. Publish it.

Read and Respond

Ask your friend to read your blog post. Ask him/her to write a comment in response.

A Watch and listen. How will *Buddies 4U* help new students?

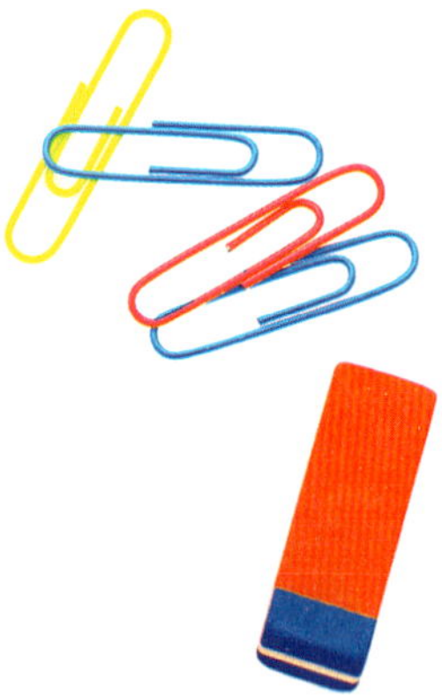

Watch
How do the slides help the presentation?

B Watch again. Check (✔) the phrases you hear. Then write *R* (cause-and-effect reasoning) or *SP* (sounding positive).

1 ✔	… had great results …	SP		6 ◯	For this reason …	______
2 ◯	… because of that …	______		7 ◯	As a result …	______
3 ◯	… this great program …	______		8 ◯	Another benefit of …	______
4 ◯	… so that …	______		9 ◯	… you'll be inspired …	______
5 ◯	… it's a great help …	______		10 ◯	… therefore …	______

C You're going to talk to your class about a new student program or club in your school. Plan your presentation with a friend.

Benefits for school:

Benefits for members:

Benefits for you:

Responsibilities:

Time in school day:

D Practice with your friends. Then share with the class. Take notes and give feedback.

Reflect
Did we use cause-and-effect reasoning and sound positive?

How well did you meet the challenge of Unit 10? Read and respond.

Looking Back

My favorite activity was …

One thing I learned is …

I'll never forget when …

The funniest moment this month was when …

UNIT 9 UNIT 10

SOLVE A PROBLEM!

Student A Problem: Poor leadership

Consequence = *If …*

Future: They need to choose someone with good leadership qualities. Say what leadership qualities the club needs.

Student C Problem: One person's ideas dominated

Consequence = *If …*

Future: Make sure decisions are collaborative.

Student B Problem: Wrong decisions were made about which sports to offer

Consequence = *If …*

Future: Have a process for making decisions. Describe what that process will be.

Student D Problem: People weren't committed, passionate, or motivated enough

Consequence = *If …*

Future: Invite a special role model to the event to inspire everyone. Say who and what effect this will have and how this will help.

HOW TO PLAY

You recently held a Special Training Day at your Sports Club to help raise money for the annual club trip. Unfortunately, it wasn't as successful as you'd hoped. You now need to plan for next year.

1 Look at the pictures. Discuss with your friends in groups of four what went wrong and what you can do in the future to make the event better.

2 Allocate a role card to each person in your group. Look at your role card. Cover the other role cards. Talk about the information on your card.

3 At the end of your discussion, vote on who explained their card the best. That person is the winner! Then, decide which solution you will choose for the future.

Process Writing

Generating Ideas

When we want to think of ideas, we need our minds to be free to write all our thoughts down. We can put our ideas into **groups** to make sure we look at all the **different parts** of the topic.

A Think and discuss. Look at the different ways we can get ideas. Which one(s) could be helpful for each type of writing? (a–e)

1 Research: question words

- Who?
- Why?
- What?
- Where?
- When?
- How?

2 Discovery

- Describe
- Compare
- Associate with
- Analyze
- Apply
- Argue for/against

3 Mind map

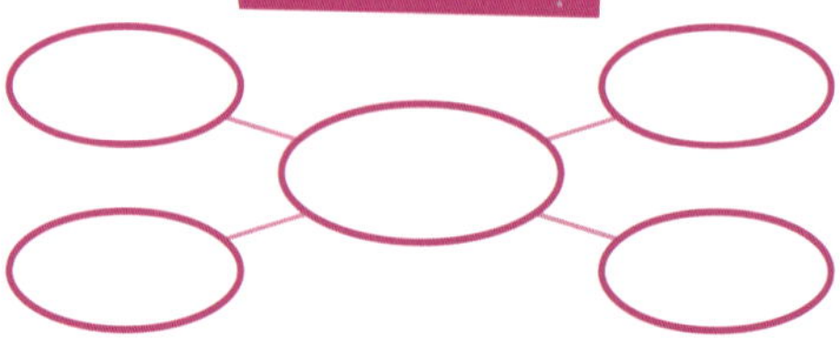

4 Flow chart

5 Categories

Pros	Cons

a. a cause and effect article
b. an advantages/disadvantages article
c. a blog post
d. a story
e. an opinion essay

B You're going to write an article called *The Good and Bad Points About Getting Older.* Choose two ways from **A** to get ideas. Make notes.

C Think and discuss. Which way do you prefer? Why?

D Write a paragraph for the article on the good points about getting older. Use your notes from your preferred method in **B**.

You can use different kinds of brainstorming techniques for different kinds of writing.

Planning

To **organize** our ideas, we need to decide which ideas are the most important. We then need to decide on the **best order** for our ideas. We also need to think about who our **reader** is and what our reader needs to **know**.

A You're going to write a story called *A Time When I Changed My Mind*. Choose a way from p. 140 to develop ideas and make notes.

Setting	Characters	Problem

B Look at your notes and choose the ideas or events you want to include. Discuss your decisions with a friend. Give reasons why these ideas or events are important.

C Think about the best order for your ideas. Choose two ways to help you plan your story. Which method do you prefer?

1 Flow chart

1

2

3

2 Sticky notes

3 Numbering ideas

1
2
3

The planning stage can be as important as the writing. Take your time to experiment with different plans.

D Now think about your reader. How can you help him/her understand the order and importance of the events and how the characters feel? Look at your story plan so far and make notes.

Time phrases	Adjectives showing feelings and reactions
then	surprised

E Write the first paragraph of your story.

Drafting

We need to follow our plan and write a first draft. Then, we look at our first draft to see which ideas work **best** and if we want to **change** anything. Next, we **revise** our first draft by making any necessary improvements and changes.

A You're going to write an essay called *Why It's Important to Try New Things*. Think of ideas and make notes on these two different points of view.

1 You're someone who tried something new and was successful. You think it's very important to try new things.

2 You're someone who tried something new and failed. But you still think it's important to try new things.

B Plan your essay like on p. 141. Then write a draft conclusion for point of view 1 and a draft conclusion for point of view 2.

C Choose one of your conclusions from **B**. How can you improve it? Think and discuss with a friend.

Add or remove information/ideas	• Is something important missing, like a reason? • Have you repeated any information? • Have you written anything that is not related to your main point?
Reorganize my ideas	• Have you put your ideas in the best order? • Do your most important ideas come first?
Change some words or phrases	• Can you use more persuasive language? • Have you repeated any words or phrases?
The ending	• Do you have a strong closing statement? • Have you summarized your main point?

D Revise and rewrite your conclusion from **C**.

We don't have to be tidy or accurate when writing a draft. You can always revise and change things at this stage.

Editing and Publishing

We should always check our writing to make sure we haven't made any **mistakes** in spelling, grammar, or punctuation. We then edit our writing and **check** it again. Finally, we **publish** our work.

A You're going to write a blog post called *What I've Learned This Year*. Think of ideas and make notes on these things.

1 What you know now

2 What skills you have now

3 How you have changed

4 How you can continue to learn in the future

B Plan and then write a first draft of the beginning of your blog post. Trade with a friend. Check the content and structure of your friend's writing. Think and discuss.

Spelling	Punctuation	Grammar
• Are there any words that are particularly difficult to spell? • Are any mistakes repeated?	• Are different and varied types of punctuation used well?	• Are different grammar structures used?

C Revise the beginning of your blog post. Then trade with your friend again. Put on your editor's hat and answer the questions.

1 What mistakes can you find? __________

2 Is there a variety of vocabulary? Write examples. __________

3 What synonyms can you suggest? __________

D Look at your friend's notes. What type of mistakes did you make? What type of mistakes do you make most? Think and discuss.

E Now, edit the beginning of your blog post. Have you dealt with the problems your friend identified?

F Make a final copy of the beginning of your blog post. Think about how to make your writing look professional and attractive to the reader. Publish your work!

Ask someone else to read through your work before you publish it. A peer-review can help you see things differently.

Macmillan Education
4 Crinan Street
London N1 9XW
A division of Springer Nature Limited

Companies and representatives throughout the world

Language Book ISBN 978-1-380-00270-9
Student Book Pack ISBN 978-1-380-00269-3

First published 2019

Original design by D'Sign Lab
Page make-up by Pronk Media Inc.
Illustrated by Ben Barter (Beehive Illustration): 48–51, 54, 56, 59–61; Alan Brown (Advocate Art): 22–25, 28, 30, 33–35; Leo Campos (Beehive Illustration): 126–129, 132–133, 137–139; Beatriz Castro (Advocate Art): 100–102, 105–106, 111–113; Adam Horsepool (Advocate Art): 6–9; Janos Janter (Beehive Illustration): 88–90, 92–94, 96, 99; Gustavo Mazali & Tamara Joubert (Beehive Illustration): 114–116, 120–122, 125; Juan Manuel Moreno (MB Artists): 62–65, 68–69, 73; Emi Ordás: 74–77, 80, 85–87; Davide Ortu (Beehive Illustration): 36–39, 42–43, 47; Szilvia Szakáll (Beehive Illustration): 10–13, 16, 21.
Front cover design and concept by 3CD
Cover adaptation by Roberto Martinez
Cover photographs by Getty Images/Leonello Calvetti (globe); Shutterstock/carballo (boy).
Picture research by Penelope Bowden, Proudfoot Pictures

Authors' acknowledgements
We would like to thank our editors and the rest of the team at Macmillan Education and RedNova Learning for their dedication throughout the writing process. It's been a joy to work with such a great team of experienced professionals and we are very grateful for their clarity, support and positive attitude.

The publishers would like to thank: Viv Lambert and Mo Choy, Salwa Abid, Meryem Bennis, Leticia Blázquez, Angel Bonilla, Victor Cojulun, John Cruft, Silvia Díez de Rivera, Randa Farouk, Magda Giomazi, Vangelina Hernández, Quyen Ho, Ziad Jadallah, Youngkwang Jang, Faisal M'reish, Riham Almughrabi, Jackie Mustoe, Adriana Ochoa, Devrim Ozdemir, Maria Pia Ayala, Silvia Raya, Ola Refaat, Helen Sharbain, Sana Sifri, Esra Tosun, Lemmy Trujillo, Tamer Victor, Jake Whiddon, Sandra Wu, Amanda Zhang, Colegio Buckingham and Gabriela Rodríguez, Colegio Euterpe and Angélica Sánchez, Colegio Héroes Mexicanos and Marcelo Carlos Hernández Morales, Internaciones Campus Fraijanes and Ana Monica Thomas, New Victoria International College and Ghada Hassan Mokbel, The Southern Cross School and Dayana Acevedo, Antonia Lira, and Paula Jorquera, Verbo Quetzaltenango and Cindy Steicy Ixchiu Velásquez

The authors and publishers would like to thank the following for permission to reproduce their photographs:

123RF/Paul Brighton p26(11), 123RF/Wilm Ihlenfeld p92(7); **Alamy Stock Photo**/blickwinkel p49(tl), Alamy Stock Photo/Cultura Creative (RF) p46(boy), Alamy Stock Photo/DustyDingo p40(3), Alamy Stock Photo/Gavin Hellier/robertharding p58(tc), Alamy Stock Photo/jvphoto p82(l), Alamy Stock Photo/Dale O' Dell p55, Alamy Stock Photo/OJO Images Ltd p40(main image), Alamy Stock Photo/Peace p104(3), Alamy Stock Photo/Rawpixel Ltd p14, Alamy Stock Photo/Alex Segre p26(9); **Getty Images**/Colin Anderson p78(main image), Getty Images/CHRISTOPHE ARCHAMBAULT/Staff p41, Getty Images/Barcroft Media/Contributor p93, Getty Images/Compassionate Eye Foundation/Martin Barraud p136(tc), Getty Images/Biddiboo p104(main image), Getty Images/BJI/Blue Jean Images p67(l), Getty Images/Luís Henrique Boucault p105, Getty Images/Kelly Bowden p124(icecream), Getty Images/BrianAJackson p124(palette), Getty Images/Kathy Collins p72(tc), Getty Images/kali9 p92(6), Getty Images/Darren Dao/EyeEm p26(4), Getty Images/Vanessa Davies p118(5), Getty Images/Danita Delimont p52(main image), Getty Images/Yvonne Duivenvoorden p26(2), Getty Images/Sam Edwards pp36(4), 38(r), Getty Images/Eric Raptosh Photography p118(3), Getty Images/fcafotodigital p26(main image), Getty Images/GM Visuals p92(5), Getty Images/JGI/Jamie Grill p32(woman,boy), Getty Images/Klaas van Haeringen/Buiten-beeld/Minden Pictures p100(3), Getty Images/Brian Hagiwara p26(1), Getty Images/Henn Photography p37(6), Getty Images/Hero Images pp40(4), 130(4, 5), Getty Images/Imgorthand p40(6), Getty Images/Hoiseung Jung/EyeEm p53, Getty Images/Blend Images - Ronnie Kaufman p37(8), Getty Images/Mike Kemp p40(2), Getty Images/Dan Kenyon p78(4), Getty Images/Library of Congress/Handout p36(1), Getty Images/moodboard p118(1), Getty Images/Tara Moore p20(tc), Getty Images/noLimit46 p78(3), Getty Images/iStockphoto/Thinkstock/Mark Oleksiy pp pp20, 32, 46, 58, 72, 98, 110, 124, Getty Images/Vishy Patel/EyeEm p52(6), Getty Images/Justin Pumfrey p118(main image), Getty Images/Tay Rees p134, Getty Images/John Rowley p130(main image), Getty Images/Chris Ryan p26(8), Getty Images/sayoga p67(r), Getty Images/scanrail p14(6), Getty Images/Friedrich Schmidt p52(1), Getty Images/Jeff Schultz/Design Pics p79(r), Getty Images/SeanShot p52(2), Getty Images/Sjo p63(tl), Getty Images/Skathi p78(1), Getty Images/stanley45 p40(7), Getty Images/Tom Stewart p30, Getty Images/Nicola Tree p36(3), Getty Images/Klaus Vedfelt p15, Getty Images/Sharon Vos-Arnold p118(4), Getty Images/Westend61 pp18, 84(tc), Getty Images/Mehmed Zelkovic p40(8), Getty Images/zmeel pp63(9, 10); **Glow Images**/Deposit Photos p26(5); **By kind permission of Julie Lourcey** p131; **Mary Evans Picture Library**/MARK FURNESS p52(3); **Shutterstock**/AnikonaAnn p26(6), Shutterstock/Andrew Astbury p78(l), Shutterstock/bernashafo p84(tl), Shutterstock/Ruth Black p46(tl), Shutterstock/Vanessa Celot p14(7), Shutterstock/chrisatpps pp82, 83(background), Shutterstock/Coffeemill p27, Shutterstock/Early Spring p20(tl), Shutterstock/Elenamiv pp44, 45(background), Shutterstock/feelphoto2521 p63(ml), Shutterstock/gillmar p62(tl:gold), Shutterstock/GreenBelka p49(tr), Shutterstock/hindersby p44, Shutterstock/HomeStudio p84(mr), Shutterstock/Hurst Photo p20(mr), Shutterstock/janon kas pp70, 71(background), Shutterstock/il67 pp18, 19(background), Shutterstock/ImageFlow pp98(ladder), 99(background), Shutterstock/In-Finity p104(4), Shutterstock/kongsky p63(5), Shutterstock/kontur-vid p124(rollerblades), Shutterstock/KorArkaR p52(4), Shutterstock/LaKirr p63(bl), Shutterstock/LiliGraphie p63(r: gold), Shutterstock/Felix Lipov p66(main image), Shutterstock/madtom pp60, 61(background), Shutterstock/majcot pp108, 109(background), Shutterstock/matimix p110(tc), Shutterstock/Meraki online p104(1, 2), Shutterstock/MikhailSh p62(3), Shutterstock/MimaCZ pp34, 35(background), Shutterstock/Moloko88 p58(map), Shutterstock/Monkey Business Images p40(1), Shutterstock/Naddya p66(1), Shutterstock/Natykach Nataliia p136(r), Shutterstock/Nearbirds p78(2), Shutterstock/Zaitsava Olga p130(2), Shutterstock/Regien Paassen p110(tl), Shutterstock/pedphoto36pm p26(3), Shutterstock/supot phanna pp134, 135(background), Shutterstock/photo5963_shutter pp57, 57(background), Shutterstock/Dmitry V. Photo p110(tr), Shutterstock/Andrey_Popov p130(3), Shutterstock/prapann pp62(c), 63(1), Shutterstock/ProKasia pp96, 97(background), Shutterstock/Prokrida p32(tl), Shutterstock/Rawpixel.com p130(6), Shutterstock/RAYphotographer p62(6), Shutterstock/Nestor Rizhniak p37(5), Shutterstock/RomanYa p119(brain), Shutterstock/Benjavisa Ruangvaree p66(5), Shutterstock/rzstudio p32(tr), Shutterstock/Scanrail1 p46(mr), Shutterstock/Serg-DAV pp122, 123(background), Shutterstock/ssguy p108(inset), Shutterstock/stevemart p62(8), Shutterstock/stockcreations p100(1), Shutterstock/Stockforlife p62(ml), Shutterstock/TairA p118(6), Shutterstock/Tashatuvango p98(tc), Shutterstock/MR.WICHAI THONGTAPE pp92(background), Shutterstock/tomertu p52(5), Shutterstock/toonbst p119(girl), Shutterstock/vanilla22 pp30, 31(background), Shutterstock/VGstockstudio p82(r), Shutterstock/ViblyPhoto p118(2), Shutterstock/Matvienko Vladimir p137(earth), Shutterstock/vvoe p62(7), Shutterstock/seksan wangkeeree p62(cl: pink), Shutterstock/Weblogiq p100(2), Shutterstock/wowomnom p78(5), Shutterstock/Olena Yakobchuk p98(boy), Shutterstock/Stephanie Zieber p62(4); **Superstock**/A. Burkatovski/Fine Art Images p66(2); **By kind permission of Kieron Williamson** p70.

The authors and publishers are grateful for permission to reprint the following copyright material: Extract from "How do children use the internet? We asked thousands of kids around the world" by Sonia Livingstone and Mariya Stoiloya. Originally published on The Conversation, 2 November 2016. © 2010–2017, The Conversation Trust (UK) Limited. Reprinted with permission of Sonia Livingstone; p. 18. Extract from Will Lourcey Frogs website. © Will Lourcey 2017. Reprinted with permission of Bill Lourcey; p. 131. Extract from "Children's cardiovascular fitness declining worldwide" by Grant Tomkinson, Ph.D. 19 November 2013, © Grant Tomkinson. Reprinted with permission of Grant Tomkinson, Ph.D.; p. 105.

Printed and bound in Dubai

2023 2022 2021 2020 2019
10 9 8 7 6 5